THE
LAST
DAY

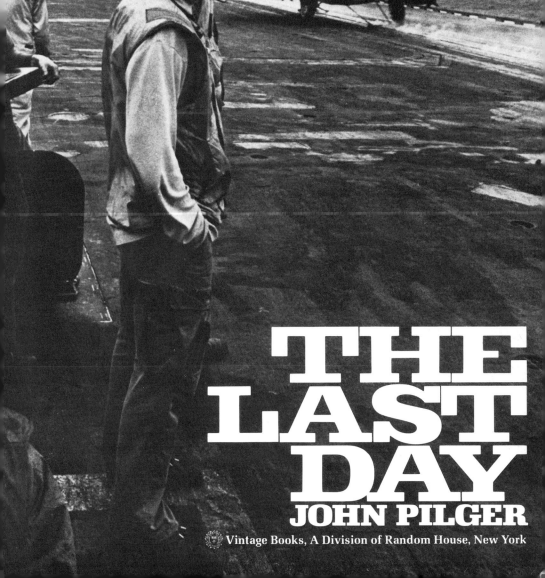

THE
LAST
DAY
JOHN PILGER

Vintage Books, A Division of Random House, New York

This book and its title are the inspiration
of Mike Molloy

FIRST VINTAGE BOOKS EDITION, April 1976

Copyright © 1975 by Mirror Group Newspapers Limited.

Pilger, John. The last day.
    1. Vietnamese Conflict, 1961–1975 — Personal
narratives, American. 2. Pilger, John. I. Title.
DS559.5.P54   1976   959.704'38   75–33212
ISBN 0–394–71643–4

Book and cover design by Janet Odgis.

PHOTO CREDITS:
PAGE 1: LARRY BURROWS, TIME-LIFE PICTURE AGENCY
PAGE 57 AND PAGE 117: DAVE BURNETT, TIME-LIFE PICTURE AGENCY

See previous page. The deck crew of an American aircraft carrier off the coast of Vietnam.
PHILIP JONES GRIFFITHS, MAGNUM

"You want to know my solution to Vietnam? Tell the Vietnamese they've got to draw in their horns or we're going to bomb them back into the Stone Age!"
— **General Curtis E. LeMay, US Air Force Chief of Staff, May, 1964.**

"We'll win! All we gotta do is grab 'em by the balls and their hearts and minds will follow!"
— **sign in the American military headquarters, Saigon, June, 1966.**

"Boys, I want you to come home with that coonskin on the wall!"
— **President Johnson to American officers in Vietnam, October, 1966.**

"Good morning! Now here's a little advice regarding our Vietnamese friends. Never pat a Vietnamese on the head. Stand on low ground when you talk to them. Make it a golden rule, okay?"
— **announcer on American Forces Radio, Saigon, September, 1970.**

"For God's sake, don't you see that once that tree falls, all American prestige falls."
— **US Ambassador to South Vietnam, Graham Martin, April 28, 1975.**

"We shall have to undergo more sacrifices, but we are sure to win total victory. This is an absolute certainty."
— **the last testament of Ho Chi Minh, Hanoi, May 10, 1969.**

PART ONE

THE DAY BEFORE

Saigon, April 28

It is dawn and I am awake, lying under my mattress on the tiles, peering at my bed propped against the French windows. The bed is meant to shield me from flying glass; but if the hotel is shelled or attacked with rockets, the bed surely will fall on me. Killed by a falling bed; that somehow makes sense; the war, at its worst, has always seemed to me a black farce. Even now, past my vertical bed in the first light outside, the absurd and venal show goes on.

Across Lam Son Square, beside a policeman's hammock and the usual pyramid of garbage, there is a young man called Flipper — brutally nicknamed that because he has no arms — and he is bellowing in English, "You got-ta live a lit-tel, love a lit-tel..." It is his only song, as far as I know; he learned it from the jukebox in the Dreamland bar on the strip near Tan Son Nhut airport, where the American contract workers and Air Force advisers used to go to be at home: to rest their paunches on the leather bar, to drink American beer, martinis and Jack Daniels, to watch flickering porn films made in Manila twenty years ago, to be massaged and fanned and touched up by tarts with steel skin and opaque eyes and flickering smiles. Late on Saturday nights, before the curfew came down to nine o'clock, they would let Flipper go through his routine: "You got-ta live a lit-tel..." followed by a little shuffle dance and a quick round with a rusted, sawn-off Diet Cola can. "Hey, Flipper Number One, eh? Money for Flipper, eh?" he would say with the Diet Cola can tied around his neck; then Randy Williams's Thai wife — Randy, from Tucson, Arizona, ran the Dreamland — would throw Flipper out. Nobody knew his real name and no-body, myself included, ever asked it. Flipper was a soldier in the ARVN, the Army of the Republic of Vietnam. He is aged anywhere between twenty-five and forty, and his arms were lost in some long-forgotten skirmish of the war. He still wears army fatigues, like most of the veterans who beg. I used to think he feigned madness just to entertain the boys, but of course I was wrong. "Flipper?" Randy used to say. "Why, he's like a mascot to us."

But Randy went last Wednesday, and the last of the boys are

THE DAY BEFORE

out at Tan Son Nhut now, taking their turn in the bowling alley and the gymnasium at Dodge City, the evacuation code-name for the Defense Attaché's Office of the United States Embassy, the former American command headquarters at Saigon airport where, each day now, more than 3,000 "non-essential" Americans and their "dependents" are being evacuated to American bases in the Philippines, and throughout the Pacific. One enormous man, an electronics engineer called Saul, left the other day with twenty-two "dependents": his wife, her parents, her grandparents, her sisters and brothers and cousins and three alleged creditors. "Jesus," said Saul, "I reckoned on taking six along, y'know, and this bunch of folks turned up. All I can say is everybody in Lima [Lima, Ohio, his hometown] is in for a surprise; now that's for sure!" Some of these Americans have paid bribes of hundreds, even thousands, of dollars in order to get passports, exit permits and tax clearances for their "dependents." They need not have bothered. Since President Ford's order to get them out, they and their flocks have only to enter Dodge City in the morning to be "processed" and flown away by nightfall. "Now hear this, please," says the loudspeaker in the gymnasium. "Each American and each dependent is entitled to one can of Seven-Up or Sprite, but only one unit per person, *please!*"

Any Vietnamese can go, as long as he, or usually she, is "sponsored" by an American. Familiar, timeless faces of whores from Tu Do Street appear in the crush, brilliantly affecting demure little expressions and wearing Barbie-doll dresses. "What's her status?" says the processor. "She's my fiancée," says the sponsor, who has been briefed on what not to say. "Okay, read this and sign it," says the embassy processor. The paper reads, "I certify that I am legally free, without any encumbrance, to marry Miss [blank space], bearer of Vietnamese ID card number [blank space], and further deponent saith not." Having signed, he now has an official, US Government-approved fiancée.

"Next . . . okay, what's her status?"

A giant called Les has an especially large peasant's conical hat on his head, four cameras around his neck, a ceramic elephant under his arm, and "Miss Nhu," a beautiful girl of per-

The consumer society which the Americans created in Saigon and the other cities and towns in South Vietnam was not entirely unproductive: it produced whores, whose work often supported a poor family of ten people. PHILIP JONES GRIFFITHS, MAGNUM

THE DAY BEFORE

haps seventeen, under the other: or as Les describes her, "the major-domo of souvenirs."

"She's my wife," says Les.

"Where's your marriage certificate?" says the processor.

"We lost it," says Les.

"Okay," says the processor, "read this and sign it."

The paper asks Les to assume responsibility for Miss Nhu "commensurate with those normally accorded a wife." Having signed, Les now has an official US Government-approved wife. "We ain't really wed, are we, lamb?" says Les, in a foghorn aside. "Sure you do, lamb," says Miss Nhu. Says Les, "That's the only English she knows, but I'm workin' on it." After receiving their units of Seven-Up, Les and Miss Nhu fly away.

These are the last of the Quiet Americans, pillars of the American empire in Indochina since 1954. With few exceptions, most of them are, like Les, middle-aged, ex-military, very fat and very sad to have to leave Vietnam. They are sad not because they love their work as jet engine or weapons maintenance men, or because they believe in the society as espoused by Saigon's politicians and generals, and for which 55,565 of their countrymen have died; no, they mostly despise both their clients and the "laziness and corruption of the Vietnamese as a race," which is how they interpret the Vietnamese refusal to swallow whole American "civilization" as dispensed by those who have devastated a third of their countryside and forcibly uprooted a third of their people.

No, these Quiet Americans are very sad to have to leave Vietnam because Vietnam gave them what they could never have back home: a cheap life, more often than not provided by the magical PX card, which was a seasonal ticket to the military's Post Exchange, an Ali Baba's cave of duty-free everything, for as long as the empire lasted. But Vietnam gave them something else even more elusive than Budweiser beer on the cheap. Vietnam gave them women. Girls as beautiful as Miss Nhu are, of course, common in Vietnam; and girls as beautiful as Miss Nhu were easily available in the towns and cities where an American was viewed as a walking bank, a means of support for a great many people, perhaps a family of twenty. And in return for this security, in times of great insecurity, the "temporary wife," the girl who went to live with an American for a price, provided a sweet servitude which not even money could buy back home.

Not all the big-bellied planes that have been droning in and out of Saigon this week, day and night, are taking out the likes of Les and Miss Nhu, and Miss Nhu's family of seven. Yesterday morning, at a quarter past eight, a sulky group looking more like evacuees from a disastrous packaged holiday than from a war, with their new Samsonite bags and hurriedly stuffed carrier bags, were "processed" separately and boarded

NIK WHEELER, SIPA PRESS

quickly. They all belong to President Ford's "endangered Vietnamese" category, and they all have one thing in common: they are murderers. American officials were not meant to talk about them, but, of course, one of them did. "Bye, bye to the Phoenix special . . ." he said acidly, watching them go, some of them still clutching their Seven-Up or Sprite. All of them had worked, at one time or another, for the Central Intelligence Agency's Phoenix Program — "program" being the nice euphemism for conspiracy. At least 50,000 district and village chiefs who were less than totally loyal to Saigon and the Washington cause were systematically "neutralized" — the nice euphemism for murdered — not by CIA agents themselves, but by

OVERLEAF: DAVE BURNETT, TIME-LIFE PICTURE AGENCY

THE DAY BEFORE

very well paid Vietnamese: yesterday's refugees. Watching them go, I wondered if the folks in Niceville, Florida, would open up their hearts to them. But of course they won't know who they are or what they did; they never knew.

7:00 a.m.

The sun has spread long spokes of thin mustard light through Lam Son Square, from the National Assembly, which the French built as an opera house, to the beautiful Continental Palace Hotel, to the most appropriately ugly statue on earth. The statue, in the center of the square, is meant to depict two South Vietnamese soldiers advancing bravely into battle, but to jaundiced eyes it has always represented an American pushing his reluctant Vietnamese ally into the fight. I remember watching it being built in less than two days by students of the Saigon Social Realist Grotesque School using "Kwik-set cement" sprayed over a swaying iron frame, with green paint added to give it a weathered bronze effect. Alas, the effect is

that of papier-mâché. It is hollow, of course. Some terrible things have happened beneath that monster: dissenters from General Thieu's wisdoms have been beaten and shot; penniless and maimed veterans have been clubbed from their wheel-

This monstrous, hollow statue (above) in the center of Saigon was made in less than two days, using "Kwik-set" cement. It was painted black and the edges were sprayed with green to give it a weathered bronze look. For many it symbolized their Vietnamese allies' reluctance to fight the American war. PHILIP JONES GRIFFITHS, MAGNUM

THE DAY BEFORE

chairs as they have demonstrated peacefully for a pension. Last Monday I watched a man come to attention beneath it and slit his throat. "His wife or the war," said a policeman, scuffing dust into the blood, "one or the other, it got too much for him."

I walk across the square to get some coffee. Flipper has gone; the policemen are out of their hammocks, stretching and lighting up; and the two loudspeakers in front and behind the monster have begun their daily, mindless clamor. For a month now they have been playing martial music and telling us not to panic. Last night, shortly before midnight, they opened up with three long whines from a siren; this, as if we didn't know, was to tell us that Saigon was under rocket attack for the second night running. Four rockets fell, and killed about twenty people. Rockets make a hissing sound, which is more frightening to me than the thud and shake of shells and bombs. They are also notoriously inaccurate. Last night's rockets, like the rockets the night before, were launched by Vietcong units encamped less than a mile away on the other side of the Saigon River. They were, it is said, meant to be "political" — that is, they were meant to persuade the new President of the dying Republic of Vietnam, General Duong Van "Big" Minh, to somehow usher the last Americans out of his country now, and to surrender.

A Saigon scene (above): a man who has cut his throat in the center of the city is taken away by police. MICHEL LAURENT, GAMMA

THE DAY BEFORE

8:00 a.m.

The Interpreter greets me. The Interpreter is a leering, moon-faced man whom it is difficult to like. When asked his name, he says, "I am The Interpreter; please come quickly." He always says this, over and over again, whether or not there is a need to come quickly. The Interpreter is a bit player in the black farce, the dream-world that is now Saigon. As recently as three months ago he was a tourist guide leading bands of mostly ghoulish people who came to Saigon to get the stamp in their passport and to take the "all city tour" which included the zoo and botanical gardens, the monstrous statue, the basilica, the covered market (where their pockets were duly picked) and the public buildings. The Interpreter says, "Some American ladies very sad . . . they come to see what their son died for, and all they see are the girls in Tu Do and these poor crabs . . ." He points to a legless soldier who has slithered out from a doorway to beg with his Coca-Cola can.

I ask The Interpreter to guide me to where last night's rockets fell, and we fill one of the minute Renault taxis which was built in 1945, the year that a British soldier, General Gracie, ordered the Japanese to be re-armed so that they could put down the Vietnamese nationalists until the Vichy French arrived to take back their colony. By this single order, Gracie precipitated thirty years of war in Vietnam.

"On your left," intones The Interpreter like a recorded voice, "is the Saigon Town Hall, built at end of the nineteenth century and a fine example of . . . and on your right, the Presidential Palace, more recent, also fine modern architecture . . . over there, typical street food sellers, selling very good little fish . . ." I ask him to cease, but he is possessed. "This now Cholon . . . colorful Chinese part of Saigon; many Chinese; Chinese everywhere; Chinese all over streets . . ." The second of last night's rockets fell near here and The Interpreter stops the taxi and pushes through the crowd along a seemingly endless alleyway. The faces stare; a few smile; for all the American years, few Americans penetrated here. "Over here typical Vietnamese home . . ." drones The Interpreter. "Please watch the typical grandmother with children, and the Buddha on the

A GI has his pocket picked in Saigon (right). PHILIP JONES GRIFFITHS, MAGNUM
See overleaf. The result of a Vietcong rocket attack on Saigon which was meant to have "political consequences." One of the rockets cut a swath through half an acre of tightly packed houses and killed twenty people, none of them a politician. NIK WHEELER, SIPA PRESS

THE DAY BEFORE

wall." This man, leading me to a scene of pain and destruction, actually imagines I am a tourist; his madness is now touching and he is no longer difficult to take. There are many like him. And as if the war is the logical end of his imaginary tour, he romps ahead, climbs onto a crumbled wall and, in a theatrical gesture, sweeps a hand in front of him and says, for the first time in French, "Monsieur, voilà la guerre!"

My preoccupation with The Interpreter's madness and my reluctance to view any more of this war's death and suffering somehow convinced me that the rockets' destruction will not be as bad as yesterday, that they will have hit an empty building or landed on open land. But no. This one rocket has cut a swatch through half an acre of tiny, tightly packed houses, and the fire storm that followed has razed everything.

There are people standing motionless, as if in a tableau, looking at the corrugated iron which is all that remains of their homes and under which there is still fire, and people. There are only a few Press here; yesterday's rockets were news, the first to fall on Saigon in a decade; today's rockets are not. A French photographer blunders across the smoldering iron, sobbing; he pulls at my arm and leads me to a pyre that was a kitchen. Beside it is a little girl, about five, who is still alive. I shall not spare the description. The skin on her chest has opened like a page; her arms are gutted and her hands are charred and petrified in front of her, one turned out, one turned in. Her face is still recognizable: she has plump cheeks and brown eyes, though her mouth is burnt and her lips have gone completely. A policeman is holding her mother away from her. A Boy Scout, with a Red Cross armband, clatters across the iron and gasps and covers his face. The French photographer and I kneel beside her and try to lift her head, but her hair is stuck to the iron by clay turned to wax by the heat. We wait half an hour, locked in this one dream, mesmerized by a little face, trying to give it water, until a stretcher arrives. The Interpreter has fled.

Only yesterday, just a few miles from here, the photographer Bryn Campbell and I staggered across another half-acre of flattened, smoldering iron, only to look as fools at Sergeant Tran van Gioi standing rigidly to attention on the wreckage of

The result of a napalm bombing raid. Napalm, a petroleum mixture which sticks to the skin as it burns, was developed especially for Vietnam. KYOICHI SAWADA, UNITED PRESS INTERNATIONAL

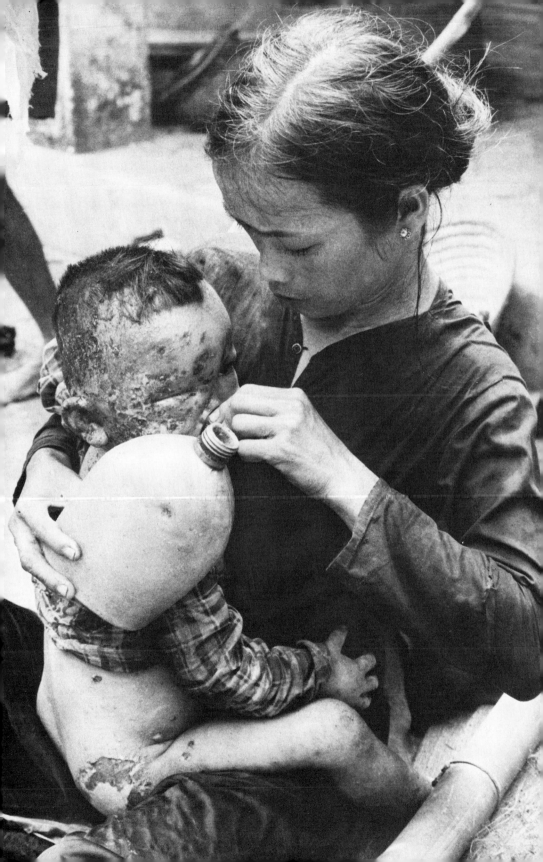

THE DAY BEFORE

his house, the rubber soles of his shoes burning, his face set like stone. "All dead..." said Sergeant Gioi in English. "All dead..."

All dead: his wife, two sons, two daughters, his mother, his sister, his niece.

Can Tho, South Vietnam, August 22, 1966

"I guess he's around ten years old," says the American doctor. "It beats me how these kids live through all that garbage out there." The boy is like an almost absent bundle of humanity, swathed in white and intravenous tubes. An American plane bombed the area his village happened to be in, because, like much of the Delta, it supplies rice to the National Liberation Front. It is a "political" bombing, meant as a warning. "Napalm B," says the American doctor. "That's the stuff made of benzine, polystyrene and gasoline. It usually sticks to the skin and is impossible to get off, and either burns the victim to death or suffocates him by using up all the oxygen. Either way, it's a slow way for a kid to die."

"Hey, hold this for a moment, will you?" He hands me the boy's plasma bottle and reaches for his camera.

"I've seen plenty like the boy, but, shit, nothing like this!"

He takes a picture of a girl who has just been carried in, her left arm charred and prostrate across her stomach, where it was blown in the same attack.

"Hey, Alice," he shouts to a nurse, "take a look at this kid over here . . ."

Alice McDonald, a tender woman from Chicago, takes a look. "Oh gee, oh ... let that be the last one, please," she says. "Thank God the war is almost over."

The drive back to the Caravelle Hotel takes an hour. The traffic is in a frenzy; people seem to be driving and riding aimlessly, three cars and a dozen Hondas abreast, blocking intersections, going nowhere. The Vietnamese, who are often open about their sorrow, are subtle and oblique in their anger and bitterness; and Saigon's traffic, where the prizes of its nonproductive consumer society are most on display, is making one more frenetic dash down Le Hoi and Tu Do before the end of all that. But just as suddenly as it erupted, the traffic subsides

This three-day-old baby girl, in her father's arms, lost a leg when the American army fired on her village. PHILIP JONES GRIFFITHS, MAGNUM

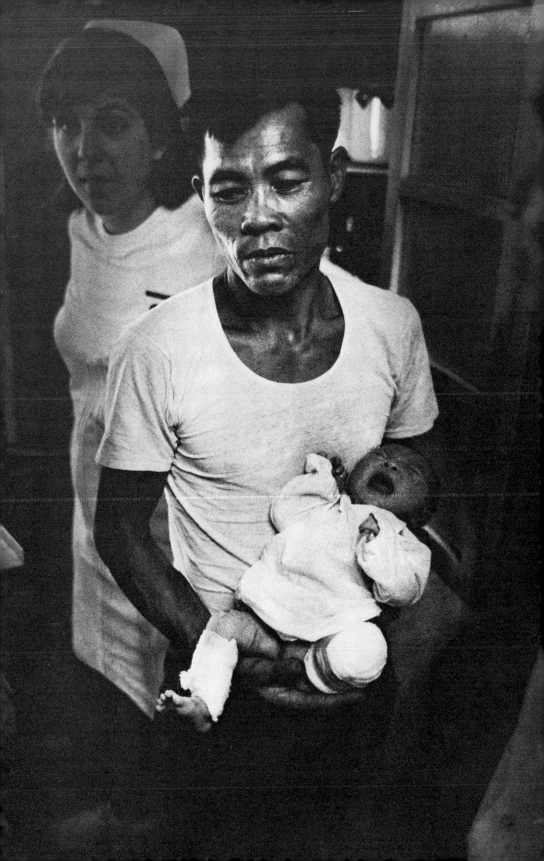

THE DAY BEFORE

and by ten o'clock the city has returned to its alternating state of dream and resignation.

11:00 a.m.

"There is no way, Tom, that I am going to have that tree brought down until it is apparent that we have lost every one of our good options. If we've got to leave, we're going to do it with dignity." The American Ambassador to the Republic of South Vietnam, Graham Martin, walks the length of the office of the Central Intelligence Agency station chief in Saigon, Thomas Polgar. As he speaks, Martin looks at neither Polgar nor George Jacobson, the Counselor. Jacobson pours himself another drink and signals for the secretary to close the door, so that a journalist, an old friend of Martin from his days as Ambassador to Thailand, cannot hear. Martin has stopped at the window and looks down from the sixth floor of the embassy to the crowd which has been at the gates since before dawn and is now being forced to the other side of the street by Military Police.

Since he returned from his home in North Carolina a few weeks ago, where he tried unsuccessfully to rest after a long bout of pneumonia, Graham Martin, a private, mightily proud and often irascible man, has slipped into a mood from which he rarely emerges. He talks with or listens to few people and instead makes statements, which, unless he checks himself, quickly convert to harangues. "For God's sake," he says, still looking out at the crowd below, "don't you see that once that tree falls, all America's prestige falls. I have given these people my word that we will not run away in the night. I have told them to come to my home and see for themselves that I am not packed and ready to go. Don't you understand that once the tree falls, the word will go out, 'The Americans have cut down their biggest tree so that helicopters can come and take away the Ambassador, his staff, a few generals and every goddamn thing we stand for.'"

Graham Martin, America's last proconsul on the continent of Asia, is a very sick man; his skin is sunken and skeined grey from the long months of illness, and his speech is ponderous and occasionally blurred from the drugs he must take every day. He is also sick at heart. Martin was Richard Nixon's man,

THE DAY BEFORE

appointed by Nixon in the last, Watergate-infested days of the Nixon Presidency for one purpose only: to keep the war alive. For as long as there was war, there would be a Saigon regime, no matter how tottering; and as long as Thieu or someone like him survived, America's and Nixon's war would not be seen by the American electorate as a complete disaster, which it was. To describe Martin as a hawk would be to attribute to that bird qualities of ferocity it does not have. For weeks he has told Washington that South Vietnam can survive with an "iron ring" around Saigon and with the B-52s laying carpets of bombs outside that ring. He desperately wants the B-52s to come back; during his recent convalescence he told a friend in Washington, "If Nixon hadn't screwed up at Watergate, he would have bombed, no question about that."

Since then Martin has sifted the ashes of the American débâcle for anything he might use to persuade Congress to re-arm the Saigon forces. After the fall of Danang he told a member of the Saigon Senate who was about to leave for Washington, seeking aid, "The orphans are important. You must make as much out of that issue as you can. If we can keep sending orphans out, keep them on the front pages, we'll swing the American public back to our side and you'll get the commitment . . ."

Martin's pain now is that even he cannot completely ignore what he sees; he knows it is his job, and his job alone, to preside over the final foreclosure on an empire which once claimed two-thirds of Indochina, for which the greatest army in the history of the world fought, and the greatest number of bombs in the history of aerial warfare fell, and 55,565 young Americans died, including the Ambassador's son, nine years ago. "Listen to reason, Graham," says Polgar, trying not to sound exasperated. "If we have to pull the plug, those big choppers are going to have no place to land if that tree is still there. Simple as that. If that tree doesn't go, a lot of our people are going to get trapped and maybe some of them are going to get killed."

The tree, one of many mighty tamarinds planted by the French a century ago, dominates the lawns and garden outside the embassy's main foyer. The only other open space big

THE DAY BEFORE

enough for a helicopter to land has the swimming pool in the middle of it, and the helipad on the embassy roof is designed only for the small Huey helicopters. If "the plug is pulled" (a term used by officials in both Washington and Saigon) and "Option Four" (a helicopter evacuation) is called, only the Marines' giant Chinook and Jolly Green Giant helicopters will have the capability of flying large numbers of people to the Seventh Fleet, thirty miles offshore, within the course of one day.

Tom Polgar is a short, bulbous man with a fretful, permanently harassed pallor. Unlike many of his predecessors, he is a well informed and pragmatic CIA station chief and has openly despaired of the Ambassador's obsessive stubbornness. When President Thieu cocooned himself in his underground bunker beneath the presidential palace for three and a half days, refusing to resign, it was Polgar, together with the French Ambassador, Jean-Marie Merrillon, who finally persuaded Graham Martin to "go down there, get him out and tell him the facts of life." To Martin, the felling of Thieu became like the felling of the embassy tree: an Olympian matter of pride and of face, for himself and for America. Had not, the Ambassador argued, the United States Government solemnly committed itself to Thieu and the American taxpayer given him billions of dollars? Had not his own son died so that Thieu's South Vietnam could remain "free"? He almost never mentioned his son's death, but it had come up in conversations in the last few weeks. The son who died was Martin's favorite, a football-loving, apolitical, all-American boy; his other son is a hippie.

Polgar listened to Martin patiently, then persuaded him to go to the palace — Thieu was refusing to take any telephone calls, even from the American Ambassador — and tell him to resign. Martin reluctantly agreed; and Polgar, Jacobson and the deputy Ambassador, Wolfgang Lemann, made their own arrangements: the tree would come down tonight, and there would be nothing Graham Martin could do about it.

Of course, Polgar was laying his own plans. The CIA had long run its own empire within the empire in Indochina: its own army of mercenaries, its own airline, Air America, its own Murder Incorporated — the Phoenix Program — and its own

The American Army's way of interrogation. KYOICHI SAWADA, UNITED PRESS INTERNATIONAL

THE DAY BEFORE

"secure GVN people." (GVN: Government of South Vietnam.) These were selected generals of the Army, the Air Force and the national police, the Washington-trained Gestapo, whose families, bar a few, had already been evacuated to the United States.

April 19 was a busy day for Tom Polgar. He had worked through most of the night drafting an "intelligence report" requested by Washington, probably by Henry Kissinger, of the "bloodbath" in the areas now occupied by the National Liberation Front, the Vietcong. This was a difficult job, because it seemed there was no bloodbath; nevertheless there were some unconfirmed reports of killings, and these would have to do. (One of these "unconfirmed reports," culled straight from the CIA's unflagging imagination, told of particularly barbaric atrocities in Hue. The report was printed, without attribution, in several major newspapers.)

At lunchtime that day, Graham Martin received a note from the Provisional Revolutionary Government, the Vietcong's politicians, through the International Commission of Control and Supervision (ICCS) in Saigon. It said that if Thieu resigned there could be a "political solution" — a hint that the PRG might agree to the setting up of a tripartite government of conciliation and concord under the terms of the Paris agreement. Martin immediately showed the note to Polgar, who said that his information was that this was a smokescreen, that the PRG wanted an unconditional surrender and nothing less. Martin, not surprisingly, did not agree; and the matter was left there. But that evening Polgar called at the home of Major General Ngo Khac Binh, commander of the national police and one of the most feared and corrupt men in South Vietnam. Polgar offered General Binh "VIP evacuation" for himself and his family, plus a "pension" in the United States, in return for a safe passage out of Saigon for the remaining Americans and some Vietnamese, should the collapse come quickly. The general agreed; and the terrible irony of that contract may or may not have occurred to Polgar: America's last exit from South Vietnam, where so many of her sons had died fighting for "freedom," was to be guaranteed by a man whose goons had imprisoned and tortured thousands of the Saigon regime's op-

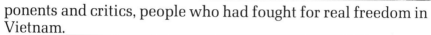

ponents and critics, people who had fought for real freedom in
Vietnam.

Beallsville, Ohio, May 17, 1970

The first hot winds of summer have begun to blow through the
American heartlands as I drive into Beallsville, past rows of
magnolias and elms and a faded billboard that says George
Washington himself farmed here. Beallsville has one main
street which is also State Highway 556, coming in from the coal
hills of West Virginia, going on to Jerusalem, Hannibal and Cin-
cinnati. It has buildings of gaunt grey and white clapboard, a
general store run by Dewey and a barbershop run by Kelly and
a hairdresser's over which hangs a sign, "Dior wigs made to
order." And beyond the junkyard is the high school where, in
two days' time, seventeen young men of the Senior Class of '70
will receive their diplomas, then stride out across the football
field and up the hill to where the Classes of '65, '66, '67 and '68
are enshrined: in the graveyard. Jack Pittman and Bob Lucas,
Charlie Schnegg, Rick Rucker and Duane Greenlee: all of them
born here and grown up here; all of them killed in places whose
names their parents cannot pronounce.

Beallsville has a population of fewer than 500. The national
ratio of Vietnam deaths is one killed for every 6,000 Americans;
for Beallsville, it is one for ninety. It is in places like Beallsville,
on the coal-scarred slopes and in the sour little hollows, that the
poorest, least known Americans live. Less than three per cent of

THE DAY BEFORE

the boys go to college; the rest go to the mines and to the war in Vietnam.

When Bob Lucas's body came home to Beallsville last year and everyone filled the streets for his funeral, Keith Harper got up and said very angrily, "Enough is enough! The way they're decimating our boys just isn't right." Keith Harper is Beallville's undertaker and has buried all five boys. The day after the Lucas funeral he called up the County Treasurer, Ray Starkey, and said, "Ray, you gotta do something." And Starkey called up Congressman Clarence E. Miller, who said he would see if he could get the boys moved around the war zone a little bit "so this kinda thing won't happen again right away." And Congressman Miller called the Pentagon, who told him, in effect, to mind his business.

Jack Pittman, aged nineteen, was the first to die. Jack was an only child and lived with his parents in a two-story gabled house opposite their peach orchard. Since Jack died in July, 1966, his mother has left his room as it was and she and Earl seldom go upstairs. These days Earl Pittman works the afternoon shift at a nearby aluminum plant, because the price of peaches has not changed for twenty years; the plant is owned by a company that makes shells for Vietnam. On March 18, 1966, Jack wrote home,

The Pittmans (above) with a photograph of their son Jack, who was killed in Vietnam in 1966. He was one of six sons of Beallsville, Ohio, who died in Vietnam. MATT HERRON
The graveyard (right) overlooking the high school in Beallsville, Ohio, where six former students are buried, all killed in Vietnam. For its size, Beallsville lost more sons in the war than any town in America. MATT HERRON

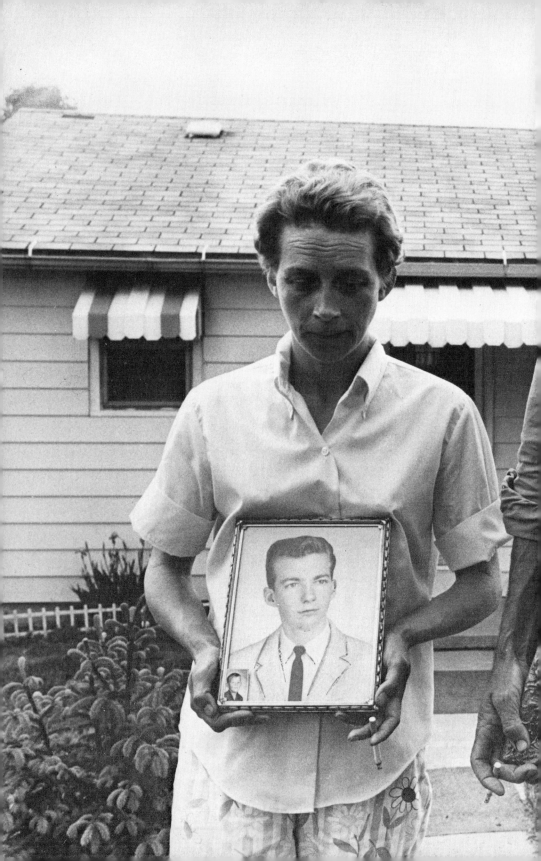

1021A EDT JUN 2 68

The filing time shown in the date line on domestic telegrams is LOCAL TIME at point of origin. Time of receipt is LOCAL TIME at point of destination

=WASHINGTON DC 1 1012P EDT

WUY7627-130 CT LLC79 (CT WA038) XV GOVT CAS PDB =

KENNETH W RUCKER DONT PHONE DONT DLVR BTWN 10PM AND 6AM

RTE 3 BEALLSVILLE OHIO (RTE ACG)

=THE SECRETARY OF THE ARMY HAS ASKED ME TO EXPRESS HIS DEEP REGRET THAT YOUR SON, SPECIALIST FOUR RICHARD L RUCKER DIED IN VIETNAM =OF 30 MAY 1968 AS A RESULT OF WOUND RECEIVED WHILE ON COMBAT OPERATION WHEN HIT BY A FRAGMENT FROM A FRIENDLY ROCKET FIREST AT HOSITLE FORCES, PLEASE ACCEPT MY DEEPEST SYMPATHY. THIS CONFIRMS PERSONAL NOTIFICATION MADE BY A REPRESENTATIVE OF THE SECRETARY OF THE ARMY

KENNETH G. WICKHAM,
MAJOR GENERAL, USA, F65
THE ADJUTANT GENERAL.

WU1201 (R2-65)   THE COMPANY WILL APPRECIATE SUGGESTIONS FROM I'

"They gave me a machine gun and a .45 today. I'm not sure what I'm to do, Mom, because I'm only a radio man . . ." That afternoon he was ambushed and shot in the head.

"The first news we had was a telegram saying he had been critically wounded," says Mrs. Pittman, "then nothing for a whole week. Why, Earl and I nearly went insane, so I said, 'I'm going to call Washington.' Well, the man on the phone at the Pentagon just said to me, 'Listen, lady, I can't trace every kid who's got himself hurt.' Well, the next thing a sergeant came around and told us Jack had died in an army hospital in San Francisco. To tell you the truth, I'd never heard of Vietnam when Jack was called to the draft. I thought it was somewhere near Panama . . . real close and threatening."

A mile and a half away from the Pittmans', in a trailer off Rural Route One, live Kenneth and Betty Rucker, whose son Rick, also nineteen, was killed on May 30, 1968. "Bernie Decker, who runs the gas station, brought the telegram," says Mr. Rucker, an electrical linesman. "Bernie's had two boys out there and I knew by the look of him what it was. The telegram said Rick had been killed by a 'friendly' rocket while storming a Vietcong bunker . . . hell, I still don't know what to believe." At their son's

See previous page. Kenneth and Betty Rucker, of Beallsville, Ohio, with memories of their son Richard, who was killed in Vietnam in June, 1968. MATT HERRON

This is the telegram (above) which Kenneth and Betty Rucker received in Beallsville, Ohio, telling them that their son Richard had been killed in Vietnam by a "friendly rocket."

MATT HERRON

THE DAY BEFORE

funeral the Ruckers met a buddy of Rick's, who had been with him when he died. There was no Vietcong bunker, he told them, ". . . just a bunch of grunts sitting around eating chow when one of our guys accidentally lobbed some mortar in and blew them all up. That kind of thing happened all the time." Rick Rucker was delivered home in a plain wooden box marked in heavy type, UNVIEWABLE, and THIS WAY UP.

2:00 p.m.

The frenetic traffic has returned. I meet Sandy Gall of Independent Television News, London, in the lobby of the Caravelle Hotel. He has the dusty, scorched look of one who has been "up the road," looking at the war. "They're three miles away," he says, "they're on Newport Bridge. Yes, I saw the flag." I wave down a vintage Renault taxi and immediately recognize the driver; it is Tran, the same cackling man who used to drive me to the Reuter office and run a finger across his throat whenever we passed the presidential palace. He is a Buddhist, a supporter of "Big" Minh, and he hated Thieu to the death. But now he is subdued and nervous, and keeps glancing in his rear-view mirror, trying to build words and courage for a question he wants to ask me. "VC in Saigon now, right?" he says.

"Yes," I reply, "they're in Saigon."

More nervous silence.

"So they take over soon, right?"

"Yes."

"Please tell me, what become of me, a Buddhist, a taxi man, always driving Americans . . . please, what happen to me; they hurt me, eh?" The rear-vision mirror shows a tough, guttered, nicotine-stained face now suddenly soft, and afraid. I hold him on the shoulder and say to him what I cannot guarantee. "No one's going to hurt you. Don't be afraid."

It does not seem possible: Newport Bridge, over which I have travelled to Bien Hoa and beyond countless times, just half an hour from the center of Saigon, now the front-line.

"Out, out!"

Mortars are landing a few dozen feet away and, in his frozen fear, Tran puts the little Renault into a culvert where, I suspect,

THE DAY BEFORE

it may die of a broken back. Crouched behind it, I am able to see them clearly and for the first time in ten years: bush hats and black pajamas and bandoliers of ammunition: infantry-men of the National Liberation Front. There is less than a com-pany of them, perhaps two platoons; they have set up mortar on the other side of the bridge, but they are really here only to raise the flag, and twice they have run up the red and blue with gold star, and each time it has been shot away by a determined nest of ARVN (South Vietnamese) defenders. An ARVN sol-dier, ludicrously overloaded with kit in the American style, charges past me like a fool, or an extremely brave man, and hurls two grenades at his black-pajamaed brothers on the other side. Then he drops on one knee, swings his M-16 rifle into position and is firing his first burst when he is blown away like human confetti. In old-fashioned wars, such an act would have been worthy of a Victoria Cross, especially as he had gone to rescue a wounded comrade in the middle of the bridge. With politicians and generals and colonels now scuttling the country, this one common soldier chose to die like that.

A German television crew, who are trumpeting their "vun-derfool footage," picks up Tran and me in their great winged Pontiac, but we have not driven a hundred yards before we are surrounded by a swell of people who have poured across and under the bridge, and along the riverbank, during breaks in the fighting. Some have come all the way from Xuan Loc, thirty miles away, and their suffering is like a plague; a baby dehy-drated and silent in the arms of a father whose feet are bound in newspapers, and bloodied; a family of five on a Honda, which finally gives up, spreading children and burst bags of rice in the path of others who do not stop for fear of breaking the desperate rhythm of their stride. Many of these people have been refugees a dozen times over. South Vietnam is probably the world's first nation where the "refugee problem" became a strategy of war.

Saigon, January 21, 1967

General William Westmoreland, commander of American forces in Vietnam, gives a Press conference to explain yet again his "search-and-destroy" missions. He is a square-faced man, with

A Saigon scene. SIPA PRESS

THE DAY BEFORE

ice-white skin and a nervous tic at the corners of his mouth. "I expect a really <u>tremendous</u> increase in the numbers of refugees," he says with pride. "Under our relocation project in the Iron Triangle, we have relocated 18,000 civilians from there, and we have today successfully taken out the jungle from there." He is asked how he relocated them.

"We sent in Chinooks [transport helicopters], wave after wave of Chinooks," he says, "and thanks to our fellows who hacked it around the clock, we got the people out of those insecure villages. We got them away from the enemy. We denied the enemy and we saved the people."

General Westmoreland is asked how he can be certain that everybody had been "relocated" before American artillery and bombers "took out the jungle."

"Sir, can I answer that?" interrupts an aide. "We dropped leaflets on these people, saying we'd be coming in with ordnance [bombs] and they'd better get out of there. We told them where to wait for the helicopters. They got the message."

The aide is asked how much warning time was given between the dropping of the leaflets and the dropping of bombs and the firing of artillery. He closes his eyes to think. "Oh, I'd say about one hour."

Up until this year (1967) at least two million people have been forcibly moved from where their families have lived for generations to "relocation centers," which is the nice euphemism for concentration camps.

5:30 p.m.

The monsoon has arrived early and Saigon now lies beneath leaden cloud; beyond the airport are long, arched bolts of heat lightning and the thunder comes in small salvos as President Minh prepares to address what is left of the nation. He stands at the end of the great hall in the presidential palace, which is heavy with chandeliers and gold brocade, and he speaks ponderously, haltingly, as if intoning a hopeless prayer. "Big" Minh's reputation as a peacemaker (the "Big" is an American tag; he is six feet tall) derives almost entirely from the *coup d'état* which he, some fellow officers and the Central Intelligence Agency successfully carried out against the Catholic dictator Ngo Dinh Diem in 1963. Unlike both Diem and former

THE DAY BEFORE

President Thieu (who, accompanied by a consignment of gold bars, arrived safely in Taiwan last week), Minh, a Buddhist, is easy-going, malleable and a humanitarian, though not especially bright. His one service to his people now is to prevent further blood-letting and to surrender unconditionally to the fifteen North Vietnamese divisions and numerous National Liberation Front units which have surrounded the city. But no, he talks instead of "our soldiers fighting hard" and only, it seems, as an afterthought does he call for a ceasefire and for negotiation, as if he really believes he has anything left with which to negotiate. He also is dream-like, like a very unfunny clown. As he finishes speaking a succession of thunderclaps drowns his last words; the war ends with a sense of theatre.

I walk quickly along Tu Do as the lightning marches into the center of the city. Half a dozen shops have closed since yesterday, their owners having evacuated themselves to the bowling alley and gymnasium at Dodge City, where they have paid handsomely for a place in the queue. The Indian tailor at No. 24 Tu Do, Austins Fine Clothes, is morosely counting his dollars when I arrive to collect two shirts he has made for me; he is cursing his transistor radio for not picking up the BBC World Service news. It is an unusual show of emotion for him, for, like his brothers and cousins from Bombay, who are Saigon's tailors, hotel door-openers and black market money dealers, he is the most pragmatic of men.

Only a few of the Indians have left, including a very rich man who asked Air India to send a Boeing for him, his family and friends; Air India said no, thank you. I have known the tailor at Austins for a long time, and the relationship has always been one of whispers and comic furtiveness, involving the handing over of one green note, which would be fingered, snapped, peered at and put against the light, and the receiving of a carrier bag filled with best-British Vietnamese piastres. (Britain's biggest export to South Vietnam is bank notes.) Saigon today must be what Germany was between the wars, with restaurant and hotel bills paid in "feet" of money.

"What's the rate today?" I ask.

"If this bloody radio will give the bloody news I will be able to tell you," the tailor replies.

THE DAY BEFORE

"I can tell you the news ... Big Minh has asked for a ceasefire."

"A ceasefire! My friend, you shouldn't have told me that; the rate has just gone down ... only 2,500 to the dollar."

"But," I say, "the VC will never accept it, will they? They will attack Saigon, won't they?"

He listens, with interest. "Okay, for you the rate has just gone up by three hundred piastres."

6:00 p.m.

Thunder now pulverizes the city. The tailor still counts his money; he has at least 5,000 dollars in that drawer, today's and yesterday's takings, and his Indian passport in his top shirt pocket. "Communists respect passports," he has said, patting his and without knowing what they respect. He once had a shop in an American air base selling comics, old and new, which he imported from a cousin living in Atlanta, Georgia, and he has worried if this qualifies him as a collaborator. I say I think not. He says Saigon will not fall for at least a month, which causes his Vietnamese assistant, whirring at his sewing machine behind the curtain, to laugh.

The thunder has a new sound, dry and metallic. It is not thunder; it is gunfire. The city seems to be exploding with weapons of every kind: small arms, mortars, anti-aircraft batteries. "I think we are being bombed," says the tailor, who flinches from his counting only to turn up the volume on his radio, which is tuned to the Voice of America's "Oldies and Goldies" hour. He says he is turning up the volume because he cannot hear the oldies and goldies over the sounds of the bombs and gunfire. He instructs one of his Vietnamese staff to close the steel shutters, which they do, but only after gathering in their Hondas from the street, which is now sluiced with bullets.

"They'll be killed out there," I say to the tailor.

"Then they and their Hondas will die a glorious death together," he replies, by way of a little joke.

For the next half hour I attempt several fetal positions in the rear of the shop, while the tailor counts and the Voice of America plays "Cherry Pink and Apple Blossom White." It is a

THE DAY BEFORE

profoundly witless song, but I sing along with the tailor, and I shall never forget the words. In a far corner, like a wounded bird, an old Vietnamese woman claws at the wall, weeping and praying. A joss stick and a box of matches lie on the floor in front of her; she cannot strike the matches because her whole body is shaking with fear. After several attempts I am able to light it for her, and only then realize that I, too, am extremely frightened.

The big noises, including the thunder, have stopped, and there is now only a crackle of small arms fire. The Voice of America has moved on to "Johnny is a bird dog . . . hey, bird dog, get away from my quail . . . hey, bird dog, you're on the wrong trail . . ."

The tailor is smiling.

"You are most fortunate," he says, "thanks to the gentlemen who have bombed us the rate has just risen a thousand piastres . . . but only one-hundred-dollar bills, please."

He opens the steel shutters, peers out and says: "It's okay . . . but *run!*"

It seems that all of Saigon is running, in spasms of controlled, silent panic. My own legs are melting, but they go like they have never gone, and are given new life by an eruption of shooting outside the Bo Da café: a military policeman, down on both knees, is raking the other side of the street, causing people to flatten or fall; nobody screams. A bar girl from the Miramar Hotel, wearing platform shoes, collides with the gutter, badly skinning her legs and her cheek. She lies still, holding her purse over the back of her head. On the far corner, opposite the Caravelle and outside the gallery that specializes in instant, hideous girlie paintings, a policeman sprays the sky with his M-16 rifle. There is a man lying still, his bicycle buckled around him.

More small arms fire spits from behind the monster statue in Lam Son Square and a soldier comes at us, running aimlessly, clutching a grenade launcher. This is my cue; I am in the Caravelle lobby in seconds, knocking flat the Bombay door-opener. "Good evening," he says, prone. It is apparently the third time tonight he has been knocked down in this way.

Saigon is now falling before our eyes: the Saigon created and

---

See overleaf. The American enemy, a captured Vietcong. PHILIP JONES GRIFFITHS, MAGNUM

THE DAY BEFORE

fattened and fed intravenously by the United States, then declared a terminal case; capital of the world's only consumer society that produced nothing; headquarters of the world's fourth greatest army, whose soldiers are now running away at the rate of 1,000 a day; and center of an empire which, unlike the previous empire of the French who came only to loot, expected nothing from its subjects, not rubber or rice or treasure, only acceptance of the American Way and gratitude for its Asian manifestations: Coca-Cola and napalm.

6:35 p.m.

There is another burst of shooting in the street outside and the hotel lobby is filled with worried people, some of them lying face-down on the marble. A tall man enters and steps over them; he is a Spaniard, who somehow has just arrived in the city, and he stands at the reception desk irritated that the receptionist, who is also face-down on the floor, is not available to register him.

"What is the situation here?" says the Spaniard. "I am of Spanish television and I am here in Saigon for this war. I send a telegram for a room and there is no one here giving me one." (He is obviously a big name in Spain.)

A quivering hand rises from behind the reception desk, and pushes a registration card and pen toward him.

"Ah, thank you! Please, I want a room where I can see *all* the situation..."

On the roof of the Caravelle, the war's traditional ringside, four of us huddle beside a pot plant awaiting the bombers' next pass. There are three planes and their target has been Tan Son Nhut airport, from which smoke fills the horizon to the west. "Get away, get away!" shouts a voice from behind us. "If he [the pilot] sees you pointing cameras, he may attack..." The voice has a certain authority, and belongs to a young Vietnamese who has run out of the staff quarters beneath the ballroom. I have sometimes come up here to lie in the sun and know most of the staff and their families; I do not know him. He has shooed the cooks back into their rooms. He appears not at all frightened, but excited, almost exhilarated. He is, it is my guess, a cadre of the National Liberation Front, perhaps acting

A Vietnamese boy after an American bombing raid. MEDICAL AID COMMITTEE FOR VIETNAM, LONDON

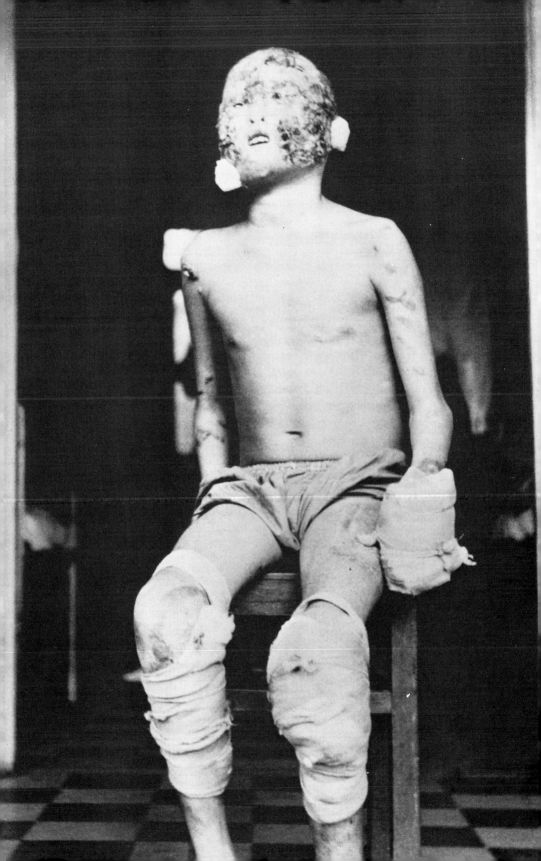

THE DAY BEFORE

as a spotter. If this is so, then the bombers, American A-37s, are booty from the captured bases in the north, Danang or Pleiku, and are being flown by North Vietnamese or NLF pilots. Whatever they are, they are probably the last planes to drop bombs on this, the most bombed country in the history of war.

Hongai, North Vietnam, June 10, 1972

The four B-52s, flying out of Guam, have levelled at 27,000 feet. Over to the south-west is the port of Haiphong; directly ahead lies the target, Hongai, described by the American military information officer in Saigon as a "major communications center." This is to be the fifty-second raid on Hongai in three days and nights, both from Guam and from aircraft carriers out to sea. Neither the pilot nor the bombardier can see anything beneath him, and, of course, they do not have to: the target is "pre-designated and pre-programed." The first "ladder" of bombs is released, then a second and a third and a fourth. Four "ladders" equal what was called in World War Two "carpet bombing." There is only light flak, and as yet no SAMS (surface-to-air missiles). The pilot banks the eight-engined bomber east, out over the Bay of Tonkin. At five o'clock this evening he and the crew will be de-briefed and at six o'clock they will go home to their families who live on the base in neat white clapboard houses with their names on the front and kiddies' sandpits out back.

Hongai lies among a thousand wooded islets in the beautiful bay of Ha Long, which means Descending Dragon, and it must be the only "communications center" in the world which has to be reached by ferry. It is not a communications center or a military base; it has an open-cut anthracite mine, a fishing port and a few thousand people.

"My name is Nguyen Thi An. I am fifteen years old. This letter comes to you from Hongai, where I was born at the foot of the Bai Tho mountain and in the murmur of the sea-waves lapping against the shore. I had just done the seventh form in the Cao Thang school. It was a sunny, glorious day and my mother had just told me to lay the table. My father had come from his work. The next thing I heard the air raid siren and I hurried to the shelter nearby. I could hear the engines of the planes and then

"It became necessary to destroy the town in order to save it." — Air Force Major Chester L. Brown, after the destruction of Ben Tre, February 1968. PHILIP JONES GRIFFITHS. MAGNUM

THE DAY BEFORE

the explosions. When the siren went again I came out. My mother and father were lying there, and my brother, Nguyen Si Quan, and my sister, Nguyen Thi Binh, were covered in blood. My sister had pieces of metal in her and so did her doll. She kept shouting, 'Where is mother and father? Where's my doll?' My street, Ha Long Street, has fallen down now. The houses have no roofs; the school and the Pioneers' Club are destroyed. This is the end of my letter."

Hongai was razed. One hundred and four demolition, pellet and dart bombs destroyed a primary school, a kindergarten, a junior high school, the Quang Ninh provincial hospital, the cinema for children and the miners' medical center. The Nguyen family's home was hit by a bomb which released thousands of needle-sharp darts. The darts entered Thi An's sister, Binh, and continued to move around in her body for several days, causing internal injuries from which she eventually died in agony. The darts were made from a plastic which cannot be detected by X-ray. This type of bomb is made especially for Vietnam.

Grand Forks Air Force Base, North Dakota, December 18, 1974

At the entrance to the officers' mess is the shield of the Strategic Air Command, which consists of a mailed fist holding a bolt of lightning above the motto, PEACE IS OUR PROFESSION. The B-52 crew of six are pleasant guys, especially the eldest, a pipe-smoking major who is the bombardier. Like the pilot, he wears a shoulder patch which says: 100 Vietnam Missions.

"Does that mean," I ask him, "that you have made one hundred bombing raids over Vietnam?"

"Yes, sir."

"Were all of them military targets?"

"Affirmative. Every one."

"No bombs fell on populated areas?"

"Negative, sir . . . except for some collateral damage here and there."

"Collateral damage?"

"That means civilian personnel casualties."

"People killed?"

"Affirmative."

Thousands of this type of pellet bomb were dropped on Vietnam. Each bomb scattered 600,000 pellets which were capable of killing or wounding every living creature within an area of one square kilometer. MEDICAL AID COMMITTEE FOR VIETNAM, LONDON

THE DAY BEFORE

"Children, women . . . ?"
"I guess so . . ."
"Did you ever think about this collateral damage?"
"Negative, sir. You're too busy doing your job."

7:20 p.m.

Ambassador Martin calls a meeting in the communications room on the sixth floor of the embassy. Everybody who matters in the embassy is there: Polgar, the CIA chief, George Jacobson, the Counselor, Josh Bennett, the head of political affairs, Wolfgang Lemann, the deputy ambassador. A communications officer talks softly to a control warden on the embassy's VHF network; he calls in the Defense Attaché's Office (Dodge City) at Tan Son Nhut airport.

"Hello, Dodge City . . . Dodge City . . . can you bring in General Smith, please?"

There is interference, and Polgar says they should stop fooling around like this and pick up a telephone and call General Smith direct (General Homer Smith is the senior US military attaché, and in charge of the evacuation from Tan Son Nhut).

"Yeah, General Smith here . . ."

Martin crosses the room and picks up the microphone. "Homer, what's the situation right now?"

"Well, it's difficult to tell. It looks like they've scored two C-130s on the ground and some other aircraft back of here. Some barracks too. Something went up with a big bang. It must have been the dump on the western side . . ."

"Lose anybody?"

"No, not as far as I can tell . . . a lot of people out here [the Americans and Vietnamese still awaiting evacuation] are real shook up . . ."

"What's the runway look like?"

"It's just fine, from what I can see, just fine . . . say, did they get the presidential palace?"

"The palace hasn't been touched. We don't believe this was a *coup* attempt. We believe the pilots may have been NVA [North Vietnamese Army] . . ."

"I see . . . okay, we're standing by out here."

Polgar and the others agree that "Option Four," an emer-

A charred body following a Vietcong rocket attack on Saigon. SIPA PRESS

THE DAY BEFORE

gency evacuation by helicopter, is the only way out now. The Ambassador thinks not. "We *must* have an orderly evacuation," he says. "We *must* not be panicked."

Martin picks up the telephone and calls President Minh at the palace and they talk for only a few minutes. Martin shrugs when he finishes. "Minh is extremely depressed," he tells the others. "He hasn't heard a squeak out of the PRG [the Provisional Revolutionary Government]." Polgar says he believes the bombing is the Communists' reply to Minh's call for ceasefire negotiations. "You can bet," he says, "that some cadre in the palace got a copy of his speech in advance." Again, Martin disagrees. "They have said they want a political solution," he says. "They're not the kind of people to change their minds when the ball game is going all their way . . ."

Outside in the compound, the great tamarind tree still stands.

It is now 8:15 a.m. in Washington, twelve hours behind Saigon. Henry Kissinger has arrived at his office in the State Department and has read the first report of the bombing. Kissinger is not among Graham Martin's critics in Washington and feels strongly that the Ambassador should make the final decision on when to "pull the plug." President Ford, however, is not so sure that this kind of power should rest with one man, about whom he has heard much but has met only once. Kissinger telephones the President and tells him that, in spite of the bombing, Martin still expects a "political initiative" from the Communists today. He then telephones his wife, Nancy, to cast doubt on their plans for tonight. They have tickets for the Noel Coward revival, *Present Laughter.*

8:30 p.m.

"Hey, here I am!" Tran, the taxi driver whose Renault fell into a culvert at the Newport bridge this afternoon, greets me outside the Reuter office.

"Hey, look, it's okay: all fixed!" He pats his venerable banger on the roof. "Axle a bit bent, but one hour to fix and she's new!"

The Renault returns five of us to Lam Son Square. I walk down to the Miramar Hotel and exchange the usual I-am-your-friend-remember-me gesticulations with the teenage mi-

THE DAY BEFORE

litia boys who, with their old Armelite rifles, police the eight o'clock curfew in Tu Do. It is now half an hour after curfew.

The Miramar bar, which sells girls for a few dollars at the blackmarket rate, is heavy with neurosis. The girls sit in a cramped circle at one end of the room; only one, the unprettiest, is going through the robot routine of stroking the vast back of an American who works for the Flying Tiger Airline and is drunk. He has a toothbrush haircut and arms like golf bags. (One of these arms recently did temporary damage to a British reporter who bravely defended, with his jaw, the Press coverage of American misadventures in Vietnam. The Flying Tiger man had said that the Press had lost the war for America. "America has left these people with nothing, absolutely *nothing*," said the British reporter, who, before being catapulted to the floor a second time, uttered these immortal words ... "At least we British left our empire with railways!")

The girls know the end is tomorrow. A few have already gone, and the others do not know what to do; such is their peonage to the rodent-faced man in the corner, the hotel pimp, who apparently intends to do business until the very last minute. Many of the girls are new whores and some have yet to wear the painted death mask of the girls who used to call out to GIs in Tu Do, "Hey, you come my house ... no like me ... like brother maybe ... no want? Then fuck you!" Even Philip Jones Griffiths, the Welsh photographer who brilliantly captured the acid melancholy in these faces, and whose pictures are reproduced in this book, might have difficulty with the latest Miramar crop, who look so ordinary, as if they have not had time to grow one more skin.

The girls' friend in the Miramar is Peter Hazelhurst, the *London Times* reporter here. Peter, a very caring man, is often chided by the rest of us for trying to "save" the girls; in fact, it is he who listens to their fears for hours on end and tries to reassure them that they will be all right if only they will go home. Peter introduced me to Phuong, an intelligent and sardonic girl in her early twenties, who has tried unsuccessfully to cultivate a sour little smile. Phuong is a kind of shop steward to the girls, and she worries desperately about what will happen to them, although she probably worries more about her mother and her

THE DAY BEFORE

sister finding out she is a whore, not a waitress, as they believe. A few weeks ago Phuong was beside herself with worry; her sister, a nurse, had arrived in Saigon and wanted to stay with her. Phuong feigned illness, the sister went home slightly confused, but the crisis passed. Like all the girls, Phuong supports a large family with her earnings — in her case, eight. Her father was killed in battle a long time ago.

Phuong is missing from the bar tonight. "She in monkey cage," says one of the girls. "She very unhappy, very scared, like all of us." The "monkey cage" is an attic room next to the hotel laundry. It is about twenty feet square and it is where the girls stay through the curfew if they have not gone to a client's room for the night. On a slow night, when most of them have to go back to the monkey cage after the bar closes at one o'clock, there is sleeping room for only a few; the others must crouch in a corner, some of them still in their paint and doll's dresses.

On my way out I meet Phuong, on the stairs to the monkey cage. Her hair is pulled back with a rubber band and she wears only lipstick. She says with mock-tough voice, "Not long go now, eh? Not long to VC coming, eh? Listen, I go tomorrow. Tonight, after bar, I cut hair and Luy Am . . . you know her: girl with frown . . . she and I leave Saigon. You know, I have black pajamas up there in monkey cage right now. So goodbye to you."

A dollar's worth of piastres sees me safely through the militia boys and back to the Caravelle, although I am held for some minutes, while the bribe is negotiated, by a boy who points his rifle at my neck. That I can accept such a holdup matter-of-factly says much about Saigon tonight.

Everybody at the Caravelle seems to be on a kind of high; we know we have arrived at the eve of something for which many of us have waited a very long time, though we are not yet sure what to expect. Seeing the yellow star of the NLF flying two miles away has chastened some and excited others. The photographer Jean-Claude Labbe, a revolutionary at heart, is almost singing with joy. "I cannot beleeeeeve it!" he says; and neither can most of us. After thirty years of struggle they are almost here, and one can only imagine the expectancy in Hanoi and the flow of messages to the house of the ailing Gen-

THE DAY BEFORE

eral Vo Nguyen Giap, the military mastermind of it all and perhaps the greatest general of the age; the man who defeated the French at Dien Bien Phu twenty-one years ago and now has defeated the mightiest military power of all. And one can only wonder where the quiet lawyer, Nguyen Huu Tho, is tonight. Tho's name will mean little to most people; he is chairman of the National Liberation Front, which the Americans called the Vietcong as shorthand for Vietnamese Communists. But Ho is not, and has never been, a Communist; his politics belong to a grossly misunderstood nationalism which has dispatched the Chinese, the Japanese, the French and now the Americans from Vietnam.

Ho last saw Saigon, where he was born, twenty-one years ago from the window of a train taking him to the prison at Tuy Hoa in Phu Yen province. He had helped to organize demonstrations against the arrival of the first American warships and planes which President Eisenhower sent at the request of the first American client-president, Ngo Dinh Diem, who was to later embarrass President Kennedy by his excesses of nepotism, graft and torture. For this, the CIA overthrew him. In those days the NLF consisted of Communists, neutralists like Tho, Catholics, Buddhists, liberal intellectuals, businessmen, members of minority and peasants' groups and a variety of others with a single aim: to free Vietnam from the control of foreigners and of their countrymen courted and bought by foreigners. Inevitably, the United States, by its massive presence, ensured the alienation of those who were not Communists and shored up those who were.

By a typically bizarre twist of this war, the NLF and the North Vietnamese already have 200 representatives in Saigon. Under the terms of the 1973 Paris agreement, each was allowed to send a military delegation to help supervise the peace, which of course never happened, and since then they have been virtual prisoners in their Tan Son Nhut barracks, which, by another twist, was the first American military camp in Vietnam, Camp Davis, and the present occupants have not changed the name. For more than two years now, at ten o'clock on Saturdays, they have held a Press conference, passed out Hanoi cigarettes and posed for pictures. When asked questions

See overleaf. Captured Vietcong "suspects." The Americans believed that anyone who was young and not in the uniform of their ally was a Vietcong. PHILIP JONES GRIFFITHS, MAGNUM

THE DAY BEFORE

like "When can we expect to see your tanks in Tu Do?" the senior spokesman, Colonel Giang, attempts to laugh, but seldom answers. Tonight I shall telephone him.

"Hello, is Colonel Giang there, please?"

"I am sorry, but he is occupied. Who is speaking, please?"

"John Pilger from the London *Mirror*."

"Hello, sir. How are you?" (It's the young interpreter, very junior and bland.)

"I'm fine. I wanted to ask you how it felt to see your own planes in action all around you there."

"What planes?"

"The planes that have been dropping bombs on Tan Son Nhut, within a few hundred yards of where you are now."

"I see . . ."

"They are your planes, aren't they?"

Laughter. "Well, it is difficult to say; we shall prepare a statement for you tomorrow morning."

"When can we expect to be liberated?"

"Just a minute, please." He says something to someone, there is giggling, then he comes back to the phone.

"Soon."

"Thank you."

"You're welcome . . . good evening."

10:00 p.m.

The restaurant at the top of the Caravelle is full. The hotel is occupied almost entirely by the Press, except for a few wealthy Vietnamese families who have moved to what they consider to be a safe area of the city. One of them has offered me a thousand dollars if I will "sponsor" his daughter: in other words, sign a form saying she is my fiancée. When I say I am unable to do this, he tries to push a bundle of dollars into my hand. When I refuse again, he offers me a box of rings and bracelets. When I refuse again, he tries the American reporter in the next room. Such is his fear.

The restaurant is a picture of normality; the food is not the best in a city renowned for its superb French, Vietnamese and Chinese cooking, but the *vichyssoise,* the *salade Niçoise* and the trout and sole are excellent, and there is wine. As we eat, a window bangs open and the curtains fly in; the waiters, normally the most serene of men, struggle to shut it against the wind, but they are strangely inept and their efforts become a surreal little cameo of tonight, especially when several of us go to their assistance and the *maître d'hôtel* screams at us, "Please, we must shut it! The planes..." The window then closes of its own accord. The *maître* covers his eyes and says, "I am sorry... please forgive me..."

Most of the staff at the Caravelle are Catholics who came south from Hanoi after the 1954 Geneva conference divided Vietnam into two "national regrouping areas." They were panicked in much the same way that people in Hue, Danang and Nha Trang were panicked a few weeks ago. Through the spring and summer of 1954 the US Air Force dropped leaflets which read: BEWARE! THE VIRGIN MARY HAS FLED SOUTH. FOLLOW HER OR BE SLAUGHTERED BY THE BARBARIAN COMMUNISTS. Several Vietnamese bishops contributed stories of Communist "bloodbaths" elsewhere in the world, and the Vatican did nothing to curb their zeal, although the Pope did not confirm that the Virgin Mary had journeyed down the Ho Chi Minh Trail to Saigon. But the

PHILIP JONES GRIFFITHS, MAGNUM

THE DAY BEFORE

doubts were enough to cause a stampede, and the Americans mounted a "humanitarian evacuation," just as they are doing now.

There was no bloodbath, and the Catholic Church thrives in the north, among young and old, and yet those of us staying at the Caravelle are asked constantly by waiters and receptionists, "Will the VC harm us?" It is impossible to reassure them, for their fear has been fashioned for too long now. Last Sunday Catholic priests and Buddhist monks gathered at the Basilica, Saigon's cathedral, for the first joint service ever held in South Vietnam. Prayers were offered, in the words of one of the monks, "to seek harmony and protect and help the Vietnamese people. It would be very good to help us sufferers."

11:00 p.m.

A French woman journalist enters the restaurant trailing two children we all know well. The eldest is a heroin junkie who begs from us in the square; the other is a flower girl who sells us chains of jasmine. The junkie girl's name is Phan Thieu Kieu and I did not realize I had known her for years until the other night when Bruce Wilson, the correspondent of the *Melbourne Herald,* said, "Don't you recognize her? No, you probably don't, because she looks pretty bad now. She used to be the prettiest of the kids who sold jasmine." Tonight Kieu is in a terrible state. "Oh, mister, oh, mister," she convulses at no one in particular. "I kill, you kill, all die, all kill." Kieu is seventeen and looks ten years older. In the bright light of the restaurant, she appears more ruined than I imagined; I had seen her mostly in shadow, begging from a doorway. Now the sores and ulcers on her legs, caused by injecting herself with filthy and rusted needles, are on show. Kieu learned her addiction from a GI, one of the many who turned on to hard drugs during their time in Vietnam; Kieu is as much a casualty of the war as the brave soldier who died on the Newport Bridge today. She is hushed and comforted by the French woman and sits at a table until someone, between courses of *pâté de foie gras* and *fruits de mer,* actually objects to her presence. She and the flower girl, who grips the last unsold chain of jasmine as if it is life, are taken to a room where they will spend the night.

An American Army chaplain at work. UNITED PRESS INTERNATIONAL

PART TWO

THE LAST DAY

1:00 a.m.

Ambassador Martin strides into the office of Conrad LaGueux, a special assistant for security affairs. Polgar, Jacobson, Lemann, Bennett and Martin Garrett, the head of embassy security, are already there. On the desk are two bottles of champagne in ice buckets; more than 10,000 dollars worth of wine and spirits are in the embassy cellar, and there is a growing awareness among the staff that it will have to be drunk quickly. Martin refuses a glass; he is sick and haggard with fatigue. He reports that he has just spoken to Kissinger, who has told him that the Soviet Ambassador to Washington, Anatoliy Dobrynin, has promised to pass his (Kissinger's) message to Hanoi requesting a negotiated settlement with President Minh's government. Martin says Kissinger is hopeful that the Russians can somehow arrange this. For a moment the Ambassador seems buoyed by his own words and announces that if the runway at Tan Son Nhut is undamaged, he wants the evacuation by fixed-wing aircraft to continue for as long as possible, perhaps for twenty-four hours.

"How many people," he asks Garrett, "can we get out in that time?" Garrett's reply is precise... "There are six thousand out there now, already processed and ready to go. With luck we could get out another three, maybe four thousand. I say with luck."

Polgar raises the question of the tree. "Not now ... please," says Martin, and the meeting ends.

3:50 a.m.

Dodge City, the Defense Attaché's Office at Tan Son Nhut, is surrounded by Marines, most of them outside the twenty-foot wire fence which was electrified in General Westmoreland's day. The Marines are deployed in pairs; each carries an M-16 rifle, four grenades, a grenade launcher, a .45 revolver, a hunting knife and canisters of Mace, a riot-control gas which paralyzes the muscles. They lie on their stomachs, with rifles balanced on their pack in front of them. There is some small arms fire a mile or two to the east and the occasional crackling sound of masonry falling in the Nissen-shaped aircraft shelters de-

In the last days of the war, graves could not be dug fast enough. NIK WHEELER, SIPA PRESS

THE LAST DAY

stroyed during the bombing last night.

Inside Dodge City, in the gymnasium, the bowling alley and the cinema, 3,000 Vietnamese and their American sponsors, who were due to catch their evacuation flights when the bombing began, try to contain their fear with sleep, gentle talk, card games and trips to the Coke machine. A teenage boy plays his tapes; an embassy official sleeps at his desk; a small boy urinates in the gutter of the bowling alley; a Marine, in combat kit, stands by the door, sucking on a soda can. In the cinema, a poster advertising the last month's movie says: THIS WILL KILL YOU . . . DON'T MISS THE DAY THE EARTH TURNED INTO A CEMETERY.

Down a long, featureless corridor, through a warren of offices on the doors of which are signs such as PRIVATE: HUMAN AFFAIRS OFFICE, is the operations room. The sign on the door says: READINESS ROOM. Before the Paris agreement in January, 1973, the sign said WAR ROOM. There is a long table, swivel chairs and a lectern which is flanked by the flag of the United States and two wall-length charts. One of the charts includes a plastic relief map of South Vietnam, colored blue, pink and white. The blue represents "GVN controlled areas," the pink "VC controlled areas" and the white "movement areas," meaning contested areas. With the Vietcong less than a mile from this room, the map is still colored mostly blue. It is here that successive American military commanders have plotted the course of the war and of strategies with high-sounding, meaningless names such as "Pacification" and "Vietnamization." Under Vietnamization, the South Vietnamese were to fight their own battles, but with American arms and American guidance. Those who supplied this guidance, after the Paris agreement, were retired generals and colonels, who were not retired at all but on special contract to the Defense Department. Many of them were imbued with the old, evangelical belief that the Red hordes somehow must be stopped in Asia before they landed in California. The charts and maps in the operations room, which are illustrated in an almost childish hand, were enough to reassure most of them, until quite recently, that South Vietnam could be "saved" and the war could continue indefinitely.

THE LAST DAY

But now most of them have gone. General Homer Smith assembled them in the cinema here two weeks ago and said, "You know it's over. I know it's over. If I were you, I'd get out right now." Now only General Smith, his aides and those Air Force and Marine officers responsible for the evacuation are left. Spread before them tonight, in the windowless room where a generation of generals saw the fabled light at the end of the tunnel, are maps of Saigon, Tan Son Nhut and flight paths in and out of the airport: the escape routes.

Marine Lance Corporal Darwin Judge, aged nineteen, and Marine Private William McMahon, aged twenty-one, are sprawled on the outer perimeter of the main runway which, in the past weeks, has been the busiest in the world. Darwin Judge is truly an all-American boy. In Marshalltown, Iowa, where he was born and raised, his passion was the Boy Scouts and his dream was to be a United States Marine. He was a member of Troop 310 of the Iowa Boy Scouts which in January, 1962, convened a special court of honor and awarded him Scouting's highest emblem, the Eagle Badge. Darwin was working at Clifton's Supermarket at the time, as a carryout boy, biding his time until he graduated from high school and could enlist in the

Corporal Charles McMahon and Lance-Corporal Darwin Jones (above), the last two Americans to die in action in Vietnam. ASSOCIATED PRESS

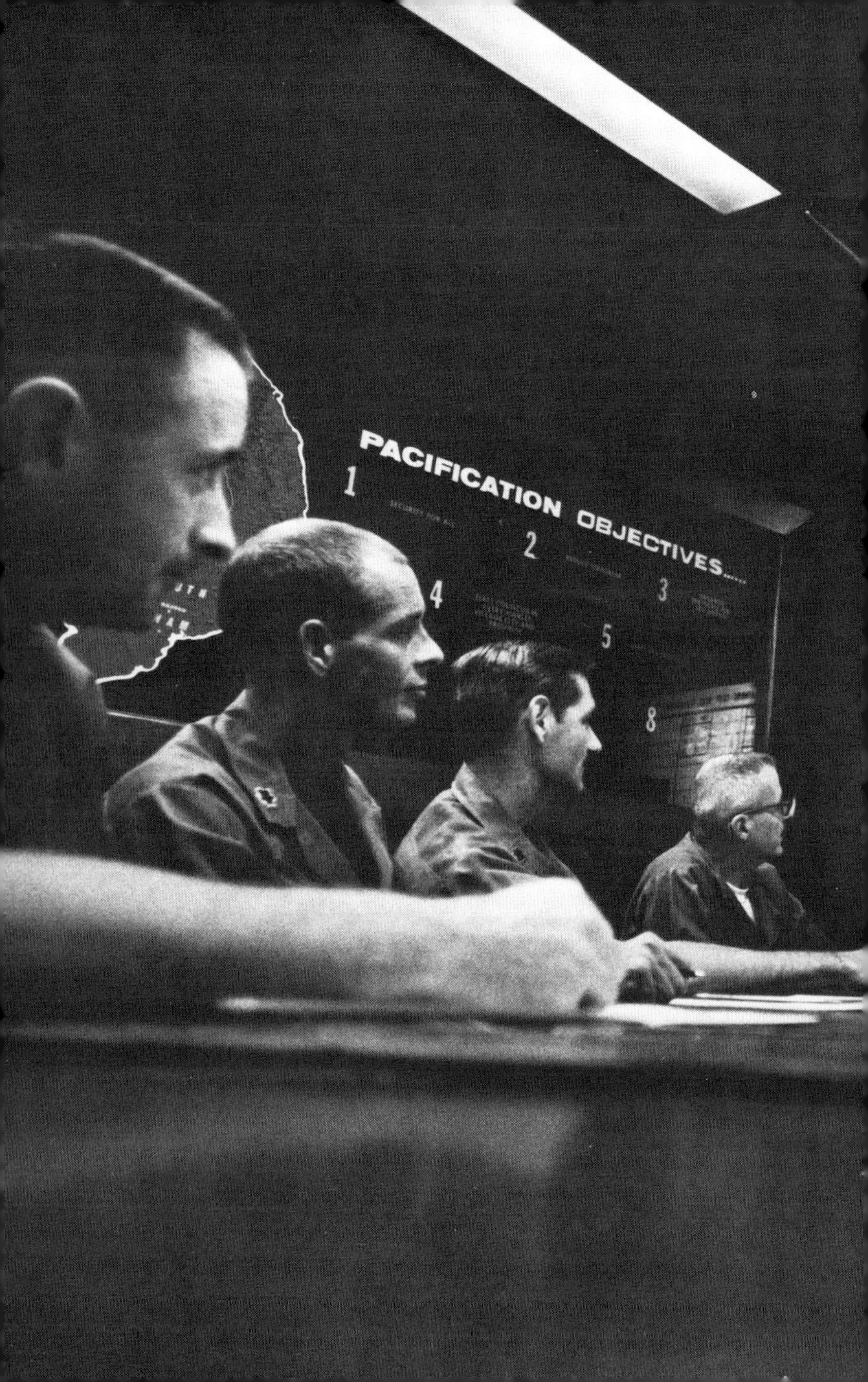
PACIFICATION OBJECTIVES......
1
2
3
4
5
8

THE LAST DAY

Marines. He enlisted last June and immediately asked for duty in Vietnam. Last month, after Darwin had sailed for Vietnam with the Seventh Fleet, his father, Henry, who is a postman, received a letter from the local American Legion which said, "We want you to know that as soon as your boy comes home, we are going to present him with our God and Country Award. We are really proud of what he is doing out there."

Darwin and Charlie McMahon have become close friends; Charlie is a similar, uncomplicated boy who comes from Woburn in Massachusetts: a town that has lost twelve sons in Vietnam, the last being Willie McCormack back in 1969. Charlie was a football hero at high school and in his graduate year he was named "Boy of the Year," which meant that he had to parade through town on a float. Like Darwin, Charlie wanted to be a Marine since he could remember; like Darwin's friends, all the folks back home are real proud of Charlie.

4:03 a.m.

"Jesus Christ! Whisky Joe ... Whisky Joe!" The voice of the control warden on the VHF network is hysterical. "Whisky Joe" is the code-name for rockets, and one after another they crash on Tan Son Nhut; there are scores of them, perhaps a hundred. They are followed by a barrage of 130-mm heavy artillery. The last battle for Saigon has begun.

From the roof of the Caravelle, the western horizon is burning. "What a show!" says a reporter. "Have you ever seen anything like that in your life?" There is a ball of orange fire, and the VHF network crackles back on the air: "Goddamn, one of our C-130s just got it ... the ICCS [International Commission for Control and Supervision] compound is burning ... the back end of the gymnasium's been hit ... my God, Dodge City, we've got two Marine KIAs [killed in action]!"

"Do you know where the bodies are?" replies Dodge City.

"Yeah, but that area's been chewed up real bad. They're gonna be in bad shape."

"Get a detail out to those bodies. We want those KIAs, do you understand!"

"Sure ... Christ, the ammo storage area's just been hit ..."

"This is General Smith. Okay, I want everybody in the gym-

See previous page. The briefing room at the American command headquarters in Saigon. During the American evacuation from Vietnam it was known as Dodge City.
PHILIP JONES GRIFFITHS, MAGNUM

nasium to remain calm . . . we can beat this one . . . if there are men on the flat out there, I want a KIA recovery detail out there right away."

Lance Corporal Darwin Judge, the Eagle Scout and winner of the For God and Country Award, and Private Charlie McMahon, the Boy of the Year, are the last two Americans to die in action in Vietnam: numbers 55,566 and 55,567.

4:30 a.m.

Ambassador Martin is awakened at his residence, three blocks from the embassy. He puts a call through to General Smith, who cannot be found; he calls the embassy, where a Marine officer tells him that Saigon airport is under full attack. He dresses and is accompanied through the house by Eddie, his bodyguard, who has been dozing in the hallway and who has to walk bow-legged because of the amount of armament he is carrying: rifle, grenades and an ivory-handled revolver tied, Western style, to his thigh. Graham Martin almost never

Mr. and Mrs. Henry Judge (above) with pictures (center and left) of their son Darwin, who was one of the last two Americans to die in action in Vietnam. Right photo shows Air Force S/Sgt. Loren Judge, 25. ASSOCIATED PRESS

THE LAST DAY

speaks to his bodyguard; as a breed they challenge his cherished independence. He telephones Jacobson, the Counselor, and instructs him to get everybody together for a meeting in the embassy at six o'clock. As they talk, the Irish voice of Father Devlin from Yeu Do Street breaks into the VHF frequency and asks if the evacuation is on. "How do I get to the helipad?" he pleads pathetically. There is no reply.

It is dawn and the sun rises as a ragged red backdrop to the tracer bullets; a helicopter gunship explodes and falls slowly, its lights still blinking, to the ground. To the east, in the suburbs, there is mortar fire, which means that the Vietcong are in Saigon itself, moving in roughly a straight line toward the center of the city, and the embassy.

6:10 a.m.

Dusk has come early in Washington, twelve hours behind Saigon, and there is light rain on the windows of the Cabinet Room at the White House. President Ford leans back in his chair and listens to reports from fourteen economic and energy advisers. Lieutenant General Brent Scowcroft, the President's deputy national security adviser, slips into the room and hands him a note which he reads while talk about oil tariffs and imports flows across the table. The note says Saigon is lost. General Scowcroft whispers to the President that Darwin Judge and Charlie McMahon have been killed, that panic is mounting in the city, that the evacuation is becoming more difficult every hour. The President scribbles Scowcroft a note which reads, "Tell HK [Henry Kissinger] that we'd better have an NSC [National Security Council] meeting at seven."

Two miles away, on the opposite bank of the Potomac, General George Brown, the chairman of the Joint Chiefs of Staff, sits on a window ledge in the office of the Defense Secretary, James Schlesinger. They, too, have just received a report of the attack. "I suggest we break for dinner now," says Brown, "it's going to be a long night." Schlesinger agrees, then takes a call from the White House. "No dinner, George," he says, "they want us up there right now."

From the Pentagon, the State Department and the CIA compound out in Langley, Virginia, the limousines and staff cars

splash through the peak-hour traffic, and at 7:23 p.m. the National Security Council, America's war-making body, meets. The President is seated at the end of the table, beneath a portrait of a granite-faced Teddy Roosevelt. On his right are Henry Kissinger, with the latest telex messages from Saigon, Assistant Secretary of State Robert Ingersoll, and CIA Director William Colby. On his left are Schlesinger, Assistant Secretary of Defense William Clements, and General Brown.

There are two "Saigon factions" in the council: the faction that has urged an evacuation for several weeks and comprises Schlesinger, Clements and Brown, and the faction that has supported Graham Martin's obstinate wish to leave only when "the Red Flag is flying at the end of the block." Martin's view is also roughly the view of Henry Kissinger, who still believes, with mighty naïveté, that the PRG and the North Vietnamese will negotiate a ceasefire; he did, after all, win his Nobel Peace Prize for negotiating the last "ceasefire" with them.

Kissinger persuades the President to postpone the order to evacuate by helicopter until they are convinced that planes cannot land and take off at Tan Son Nhut. Schlesinger, who does not sympathize with Martin's views, is extremely unhappy. When the meeting ends, General Brown calls the Air Force Chief of Staff and tells him to order two C-130 Hercules aircraft out of Clark Air Base in the Philippines. "They are to

The unequal allies (above): **Major General Ngo Quang Truong, Commanding General, 1st ARVN Infantry Division, bringing up the rear of Major General John J. Tolson III, Commander, 1st US Cavalry Division.** PHILIP JONES GRIFFITHS, MAGNUM

THE LAST DAY

attempt to land in Saigon," he says. "If they make it, that's great. If they don't, we're into Option Four."

In Saigon the six o'clock meeting between Martin and his top officials has been a disaster. All of them, except Martin, say that they should evacuate now, right now, while there is time. Martin says, "I refuse to run away from this thing," and he announces, to their horror, that he will drive to Tan Son Nhut to assess the situation for himself. There is now more than a suspicion among a number of embassy staff, Tom Polgar included, that the last proconsul of the empire, in his obsessive stubbornness, might, just might, have plans to burn with Rome. When the meeting ends in confusion, they order, without the Ambassador's approval, the great tamarind tree chopped down.

Washington, D.C., April 25, 1971

"The truth is out! Mickey Mouse is dead! The good guys are really the bad guys in disguise!" The speaker is William Wyman, from New York City. He is nineteen and has no legs. He sits in a wheel-chair on the steps of the United States Congress, in the midst of a crowd of 300,000, the greatest demonstration America has ever seen. He has on green combat fatigues and the jacket is torn where he has ripped away the medals and the ribbons he has been given in exchange for his legs, and along with hundreds of other veterans of the war in Vietnam, he has hurled them on the Capitol steps and described them as shit; and now to those who form a ring of pity around him, he says, "Before I lost these legs, I killed and killed! We all did! Jesus, don't grieve for me!"

All week the veterans have been in Washington. Never before in this country have young soldiers marched in protest against the war they themselves have fought and which is still going on. They have stopped Mr. and Mrs. America in the street and told them about the gore and what they did, which they describe as atrocities. They have marched, or tried to march, a battalion of shuffling stick figures, to the Department of Defense, where they have tried to give themselves up, only to be told by a bemused one-star general, "Sorry, we don't take American prisoners here."

On April 25, 1971, more than 300,000 people came to Washington to protest against the war in Vietnam. Among them were veterans like William Wyman, who lost both legs in Vietnam. These young veterans went to the steps of the Capitol and hurled down their medals and decorations. BILL VETELL

THE LAST DAY

Dale Grenada, a former quartermaster on a destroyer, shouting through a bullhorn, describes to rush-hour shoppers how he helped to raze a Vietnamese village: "Listen to this, friends . . . the whole village was burning but the spotter planes reported people fleeing across the open fields, so we switched to fragmented shells and began to chop the people up. Then we began firing phosphorus shells and watched them burn."

The veterans' presence in Washington today is deeply confusing to the American mood. A police sergeant on duty at the Capitol says, "Hell, I'd throw in my badge before I touch these guys." A businessman, who was just passing by, now fussily clears a path for Bill Loivie, who has spent two years in military hospitals and will always need crutches. An old couple, he in red baseball cap, she in blue rinse, have come up from Georgia to see Washington in the spring and now they march with a woman who lost a son over there. Even a party of enormous ladies from the Daughters of the American Revolution, an organization that would gleefully detonate the world tomorrow and which happened to be meeting in Washington today, stand transfixed and almost crying, almost, as the carnage passes them by, including Jack Saul from California wearing a grotesque mask of Richard Nixon smiling. And when someone asks Jack, jokingly, what he himself looks like, he takes it off and reveals a face that looks as though he has just finished pouring acid on it. "Peace," he says.

7:30 a.m.

Graham Martin leaves his residence for Tan Son Nhut in his bullet-proof Cadillac. The Cadillac served the two previous American Ambassadors and its age and slightly worn appearance have concerned Martin for some time now. He believes an American Ambassador should look like an American Ambassador, right down to the chrome on his limousine; he is a man much concerned with "dignity," both of action and appearance. Last year he sent one of his angrier messages to Washington about a new car, and six weeks ago he was told that a brand new, Secret Service-approved Cadillac was on the way. Then, when the Central Highlands, Hue and Danang fell, he was told that his Cadillac had been diverted to Israel, where

THE LAST DAY

the "security needs" of the American Ambassador, the proconsul for the Middle East, were more pressing. Graham Martin was sorely offended; to him, the cancellation of his car was a signal that Washington was preparing to scuttle Vietnam without consulting him. For what other reason would they take away such a vital prop to his dignity? He sent several more messages demanding a replacement car, but they were all turned down. The Cadillac, like the great tamarind tree, had become to Graham Martin a symbol of his and America's credibility, which he calls prestige.

He is alone in the back of the Cadillac, with Eddie the bodyguard and the Vietnamese driver in the front. Eddie sits with both hands checking his armory like a man looking for a lost wallet. Eddie's favorite expression is "I'm pissed." Eddie has never been more pissed than he is now because the Ambassador has refused a Marine escort, which means only he can prevent the unthinkable.

The anxious voice of Jacobson, the Counselor, comes on the VHF network: "Tell the Ambassador to proceed with utmost caution. There's some incoming fire between the road and the DAO [Defense Attaché's Office] . . . a bus has been hit . . ."

A rocket falls a few hundred yards from the Cadillac, and there is some small arms fire from ARVN soldiers in the distance, but Martin tells the driver to proceed. Jacobson says something to the effect that the American Ambassador ought not to be the last American to die in Vietnam, and some of this is picked up on the network, to which most of Saigon's Press corps is listening. Martin does not reply.

At Tan Son Nhut he is met by General Smith and they survey the damage, as best they can, from a jeep. Martin is shocked; there is fire all around the airport, and open rebellion among the ARVN. He asks Smith for his appraisal. Smith says, "Either we go with Option Four or we're going to look pretty stupid or pretty dead."

8:18 a.m.

It is mid-Monday evening in Washington. President Ford, hands in his pockets, walks to his residence in the White House. He greets his wife, Betty, with a kiss, throws his feet up

THE LAST DAY

on a coffee table and sips a before-dinner martini. Kissinger arrives and reports that the two C-130s are in the air and will attempt to land in Saigon in just under two hours. David Kennerly, the White House photographer who works hard to make the President look statesmanlike, asks the President and his Secretary of State to look at each other earnestly, if not gravely; this they do, with appropriately furrowed brows and pursed lips and documents held in the manner of those contemplating war and peace. Both are well practiced at this; Kissinger is the best ham; the President tends to look himself.

Twelve minutes later Nancy Kissinger arrives at the White House, in a full-length evening gown, to take Henry to the Noel Coward play. Henry says he is sorry, but Saigon is falling. She understands, of course, and will watch television while she waits for him. The President has joined Betty Ford in the family dining room, where they eat oyster cocktail, corned beef with cabbage, carrots and beet salad followed by black cherry jello. The President eats a lot of jello. (Menu supplied by the White House Press office.)

Over at the Pentagon, James Schlesinger and General Brown are also having dinner: hamburgers served at their desks. Schlesinger has mustard; General Brown prefers to approach his hamburger through dollops of tomato ketchup. (Menus supplied by the Pentagon public affairs office.) The Defense Secretary and America's most senior general then descend into the National Military Command Center, the operations center on the second floor of the Pentagon, a wonderland of red, blue and yellow telephones, blinking maps, oval table and leather chairs. The two men are greeted by a brace of generals and admirals — "Hi, George . . . well hello, WJ . . . hi there, Jim" — are served coffee by earnest messengers and settle down to listen to the loudspeakers broadcasting every American word on the tied circuits between Washington, Honolulu, Clark Air Force base in the Philippines and Saigon. There has not been a show quite as enjoyable as this since the Cuban missile crisis.

8:40 a.m.

Graham Martin drives back from Tan Son Nhut in silence, this time with a jeep escort, which General Smith has insisted

THE LAST DAY

upon. At the same time, a fleet of cars and trucks pulls into the market outside the Botanical Gardens and Zoo and its cargo is quickly unloaded: frozen steaks, pork chops, orange juice, great jars of pickles and maraschino cherries, cartons of canned butter peas and Chunkie peanut butter, Sara Lee cakes, Budweiser beer, Seven-Up, Wrigley's Chewing Gum, Have-A-Tampa plastic-tipped cigars and more, all of it looted from the Saigon PX — the Post Exchange which was abandoned early this morning, shortly after an NLF sapper unit strolled in Indian file past its rear doors. To the Saigonese, stealing from their mentors and patrons has always been something of a moral obligation, and there is a carnival air and much giggling as fast-melting T-bones are sold for a few cents.

A pick-up truck discharges a dish-washing machine and a water cooler; the water cooler is quickly sold and driven away in a tri-shaw; the dishwasher is of the Blue Swan brand and on its box is the Blue Swan motto: "Only the best for our customers." The dishwasher is taken from its box and left on the road. Two hours later it is still there, unsold and stripped of vital parts, a forlorn monument to American salesmanship in Vietnam.

Tuylon, South Vietnam, August 23, 1967

When Sergeant Melvin Murrell and his company of United States Marines drop by helicopter into the village of Tuylon, west of Danang, with orders to sell "the basic liberties as outlined on page 233 of the Pacification Program Handbook" and at the same time win the hearts and minds of the people (see same handbook, page 86 under WHAM) they see no one: not a child or a chicken. The population has watched them come out of the sky, and most of them have retired to the paddies or stand silent in the shadows of their houses.

"Come on out, we're your friends," Sergeant Murrell shouts through a bullhorn, in English.

"Come on out, everybody, we got rice and candy and toothbrushes to give you," he coos into the hot silence.

"Listen, either you gooks come out from wherever you are or we're going to come in there and get you," he jokes, as soldiers at war are given to joke.

Sergeant Melvin Murrell, who gave away 7,000 toothbrushes to the villagers of Tuylon, in order to win their hearts and minds. RAY CRANBOURNE, MAGNUM

THE LAST DAY

So the people of Tuylon come out from wherever they are and queue to receive packets of "miracle rice," Uncle Ben's brand, and Hershey chocolate bars and 7,000 toothbrushes, which come in four colors, and comics for the children — Superman, etc. — and in a separate, almost touching little ceremony, the district chief is presented with four yellow portable, battery-operated flush lavatories.

"If these are right for your requirements," says Sergeant Murrell, "there will be more where they came from." And when it is all over and the children cheer on cue, Sergeant Murrell notes in his log of the day: "At first, they did not appear to understand that we had come to help them. However, they were persuaded otherwise, and at this time they are secured and on our side. I believe they respect our posture of strength and humanity. I believe the colonel will be pleased."

The Marines with whom I have come to Tuylon are called a CAC unit, which stands for Combined Action Company, which means their role is both military and civil. First, a CAC unit moves into a village and "protects" it — whether or not the villagers have asked to be protected — with trenches and booby traps and barbed wire. Then they declare the village "friendly" and set about selling "the basic liberties as outlined on page 233 of the Pacification Program Handbook" to old men and young men, women and children.

There is, however, a problem. The United States Marines would rather fight the Vietnamese than sell them the basic liberties and win their hearts and minds. "I'll say this for these people," says Murrell, "they do what they're told. I guess it's like I always say: whoever's got the guns calls the tune."

Tuylon, one week later:

Colonel Richard Trueball has arrived. "Well, slap my mouth, it sure is good to see you, sir," says Sergeant Murrell.

"How is everything here, Murrell? How is the hygiene program coming along? Toothbrushes, toilets cause an impact?"

"Yes, indeed, sir. Toothbrushes went down a dandy but as for gettin' them to go to the bathroom and all that — well, I'm afraid these people been doin' it other ways for thousands of years and they seem to like it that way."

The colonel thinks.

THE LAST DAY

"Never say die, Murrell. I'll send you in a portable shower unit on Thursday."
"Yes, sir!"

9:00 a.m.

The tree-cutters assemble; these are the men who will fell the great tamarind; a remarkable group of CIA guards, former Special Forces men (the Green Berets), security men from Army, Air Force and Marine intelligence and an assortment of former GIs supplied by two California-based companies to protect the embassy in these troubled days. They carry weapons that would delight the collector, including obsolete and adorned machine guns and pistols, and a variety of knives. However, they share one uniformity; they walk with a swagger that is pure cowboy: legs slightly bowed, right hand hanging loose, fingers turned in and now and then patting the holster. They are issued with axes and power saw, and secretaries from the embassy bring them beer and sandwiches. They are cutting down the Ambassador's tree.

9:00 a.m.

Saigon is under a twenty-four-hour curfew, but there are people in the streets, and some of them are soldiers from the 18th ARVN division which fought so well at Xuan Loc, the last provincial capital on Highway One. We have been expecting them and awaiting the first signs of their anger and bitterness as they watch the Americans preparing to leave them to their fate. This morning, when they first appeared in the center of the city, they merely eyed foreigners, or robbed them, or fired into the air to relieve their frustration.

I have asked Tran the taxi driver to come for me at nine o'clock, because I have received a desperately worded message from a Vietnamese doctor at the Tu Duc Hospital, whom I have known for almost as long as I have been coming here. It was he who gave me information in 1969 about the effects of the chemical war on people and particularly on pregnant women. The chemical war was the systematic poisoning of fields and paddies and the defoliation of forests with a spray called 2,4,5-T. At that time the large hospital at Hung Vuong

THE LAST DAY

reported a "fetal catastrophe"; out of 5,870 births, forty-seven had produced deformities reminiscent of thalidomide. The Tu Duc hospital is a teeming place and I went there to check this, and met a young doctor who showed me two newly born deformed babies. He said, "You see, the damage is the same, because both their mothers drank contaminated water in a sprayed area. We had an American research team here and they said the damage was caused by an impurity in the spray called dioxin. I asked them to send me their report, but it didn't come."

Two months later the National Cancer Institute in Washington confirmed that 2,4,5-T contained dioxin, the most powerful fetal-deforming substance known to chemists and many times stronger than thalidomide. The Institute's report caused an immediate ban on the spray, which was made by the Dow Chemical Company, the napalm people, but the ban did not apply to Vietnam. Instead, the public affairs office of the US command in Saigon demonstrated that it was not entirely insensitive to the issue and changed the name of the "defoliant program" from Operation Hades to the more friendly Operation Blue Skies and Operation Ranch Hand. Two weeks ago the same doctor showed me yet another deformed baby and said that they were common now.

He is waiting for me at the hospital entrance and says immediately, "Please, can you write this in your newspaper? It is terrible, disastrous. All but two of our surgeons have left . . . just left, yesterday and today. One of them walked out from an operation. We have patients who will die unless they are operated on . . . you must appeal to these men and make them come back . . ."

9:55 a.m.

The two C-130s from the Philippines are over Tan Son Nhut now. The pilots' voices are heard clearly in the National Military Command Center in Washington. They request orders. General Smith, at the Dodge City radio control, tells them that "things might be a little rough down here" and instructs them to drop to 16,000 feet and to start their fourteen-minute approach. Smith, and most of the military command listening in

THE LAST DAY

Washington, are incensed that the President has refused their request for a fighter escort for the C-130s on the grounds that Congress may not approve. But they say nothing; in the White House, the President and Kissinger are listening to every word.

9:45 a.m.

I return to the Caravelle and call at Sandy Gall's room; Sandy and I are the unofficial evacuation wardens for the "TCN Press"; TCN is an American term meaning Third Country Nationals, which means anyone who is not American or Vietnamese. For some days now, Sandy and I have concerned ourselves with the supremely eccentric task of trying to organize those of the British, Canadian, Italian, German, Spanish, Argentinean, Brazilian, Dutch and Japanese Press who want to be evacuated. The American Embassy has distributed a fifteen-page booklet called SAFE — short for Standard Instruction and Advice to Civilians in an Emergency. The booklet includes a map of Saigon pinpointing "assembly areas where a helicopter will pick you up." It says there will be four color-coded alerts: white, grey, yellow and red. When the red alert comes, it is everybody to the assembly points and, I quote, "you should bring along two changes of clothing, a raincoat, a sewing kit, an umbrella, a can opener, insect repellent, your marriage certificate, a power of attorney and your will . . . but unfortunately you must leave your furniture and your automobile behind." There is an insert page which reads, "Note evacuation signal. Do not disclose to other personnel. When the evacuation is ordered, the code will be read out on American Forces Radio. The code is:

THE TEMPERATURE IN SAIGON IS 112 DEGREES AND RISING. THIS WILL BE FOLLOWED BY THE PLAYING OF "I'M DREAMING OF A WHITE CHRISTMAS."

Presumably it will be Bing Crosby's version. Philip Jacobson, of the *Sunday Times*, says the Japanese journalists are very worried about whether they will recognize the tune and are trying to find someone to sing it for them.

At the Caravelle, Gall and I have delegated floor wardens who, on the signal to evacuate, will ensure that reporters who are infirm, deaf, asleep, confined in the lavatory or to a liaison,

THE LAST DAY

will not be left behind. Our original master plan was to bring in a chartered Boeing from Hong Kong or Bangkok. It sounded almost perfect at the time; we would not have to leave with the Americans. But of course it was pregnant with doom and, as it turned out, the civilian aviation authorities in Washington declared Saigon airport unsafe to commercial aircraft and any company doing business with us would risk losing its license.

I return to my room to write and pass Michel Laurent's room, which is as he left it five days ago. Michel drove to Bien Hoa, where there was fighting, and has not been heard from. There is a report that his car was hit by a rocket and that he was seen lying nearby, wounded. Michel is a very fine photographer for the Gamma agency in Paris who has produced some of the most searing pictures of the war, not of battles but of the agony of civilians. He came back to Vietnam reluctantly; he was Gamma's only man with a valid visa in his passport. He is a thin, gentle, freckled man who seldom wears combat kit when he is covering the war, but who probably takes more risks than most of us. Over dinner the other night he said, "I take pictures of wars for the simple reason that I want people never to forget how *horrible* they are ..."

10:12 a.m.

The C-130s are four minutes away from touch-down, but General Smith is on the radio telling them not to land. The scouts he sent to the perimeter of the airport have returned with the report that two platoons of North Vietnamese infantry have reached a cemetery half a mile away; and a few minutes ago a South Vietnamese pilot landed his F-5 fighter on the runway and abandoned it with its engine running, and a jeep-load of ARVN are now ramming one of their own C-130s as it prepares to take off. "There are some three thousand panicking civilians on the runway," says General Smith on the radio. "The situation appears to be out of control." He immediately calls Admiral Gaylor in Honolulu and says that, in his opinion, "the helicopter evacuation should begin now ... or I don't know what!"

The conversation is heard in both the National Military Operations Center at the Pentagon and in the Situation Room in the basement of the White House, where Henry Kissinger is

The war had many bizarre sides. One was the presence of 200 North Vietnamese and Vietcong troops in a compound at Saigon airport. They belonged to a military mission sent to Saigon under the terms of the Paris agreement in January, 1973. Every Saturday morning at ten o'clock they held a press conference, after which the otherwise elusive "enemy" would pose for pictures (above). MICHEL LAURENT, GAMMA

listening. Kissinger calls the President, who is posing for more crisis photographs; this one will have Betty Ford in it, arms folded over a quilted housecoat, deep concern on her face.

Kissinger tells the President he is going to call Ambassador Martin; the President agrees as he is photographed, nodding, looking somber.

10:30 a.m.

General Smith at Tan Son Nhut and Admiral Gaylor in Honolulu call Graham Martin, who is alone in his office at the embassy, having just watched the great tamarind tree fall and heard his CIA Station Chief cry, "Timberrr!" Both the general and the admiral ask the Ambassador to make up his mind; Martin replies that there is still time; Smith and Gaylor have obvious difficulty containing their anger on the circuit. Martin puts down the telephone and says to Jacobson that Hanoi has sold them a line, that they never intended to negotiate. Like his predecessor, the Ambassador had believed what he wanted to believe.

10:43 a.m.

The telephone on the Ambassador's desk rings again. It is Kissinger. They discuss the events of the last six and a half hours,

THE LAST DAY

with Kissinger gently easing an exhausted and ailing Martin to a decison. "Yes, all right," the Ambassador says finally, "let's go with Option Four." (The first three "options" were evacuation by sea and by fixed-wing aircraft.) Kissinger immediately telephones the President, who orders the evacuation to begin. Kissinger then calls Schlesinger who, as Defense Secretary, must pass the President's order to the Pentagon. The order is to "implement Operation Frequent Wind." It is now 10:51 a.m. in Saigon, thirteen years, four months and seven days since the first American soldier, Specialist Fourth Class James Thomas Davis, from Livingston, Tennessee, died in Vietnam.

It is also almost twenty years to the day since the United States Office of Strategic Services, the forerunner to the CIA, began parachuting men into Vietnam to help an obscure resistance leader called Ho Chi Minh in his fight against the Japanese. It is perhaps the supreme and most forgotten irony of the Vietnamese struggle that Ho Chi Minh and his senior military commander, Vo Nguyen Giap, were among the first to collaborate with the Americans, though in a very different manner from the servility of those who took power in Saigon. For two months the OSS teams trained Ho's guerillas, and when Ho fell seriously ill with a variety of tropical diseases, a young American Army medic called Paul Hoagland filled him with sulphur drugs and quinine and probably saved his life. And when Ho walked as a liberator through the streets of Hanoi, the Americans walked with him.

12:25 p.m.

It is now after midnight in Washington and the President goes to bed with a glass of hot buttermilk. According to the White House Press office, the President goes to bed with a glass of hot buttermilk every night.

12:45 p.m.

The first wave of thirty-six Marine and Air Force helicopters take off from the carrier USS Hancock, one of forty ships of the Seventh Fleet now steaming in the South China Sea, some twenty miles off the coast of Vietnam and 100 miles from Saigon. At the same time, F-4 fighter bombers take off from the

A long forgotten irony of the war in Vietnam is expressed in this family album style picture. A young Ho Chi Minh stands in a forest glade with his Quiet Americans: members of the Office of Strategic Services, the forerunner of the CIA, who parachuted into Vietnam in June 1945 to help the Vietnamese nationalists in their struggle against the Japanese. The little man in the white suit, club tie and felt trilby is General Vo Nguyen Giap, who was to master-mind the defeat of the French and the Americans. The pith helmet-carrying American on the extreme left is Paul Hoagland, a US Army medic who found Ho sick with tropical diseases, filled him with sulphur drugs and quinine, and probably saved his life. LIFE MAGAZINE

THE LAST DAY

Utapao Air Force base in Thailand, to provide cover for the helicopters.

1:15 p.m.

Henry Kissinger leaves the White House at 1:15 a.m. Washington time and walks along Pennsylvania Avenue with his wife, Nancy. They are smiling a great deal and Kissinger says to the reporters following him, "We hope to have some pretty good news soon."

"*Good* news, Mr. Secretary?" says one of them.

"Yes, my friend, *good* news," says Kissinger, his smile tightening.

1:20 p.m.

An unfamiliar voice comes over the scrambled circuit at the National Military Command Center, ordering the helicopters not to land at Tan Son Nhut at the scheduled time of two o'clock, but one hour later. The circuit is immediately jammed with Admiral Gaylor, General Smith and others shouting at the tops of their voices: "Who gave that order?" In the confusion only the lead helicopter carrying Marine Brigadier General Richard Curry receives the correction, while the thirty-five other helicopters go into a holding pattern over the sea, losing valuable daylight time.

1:30 p.m.

I stroll down the corridor to learn the latest on the evacuation; a French cameraman says the evacuation has been called, and I, Unofficial Joint TCN Warden of the Caravelle Hotel (UJTCNWCH), have missed it. Phil Jacobson's room, next to mine, looks like the *Marie Celeste*: papers on the desk, clothes in the wardrobe, toothbrush, etc., in the bathroom. The hotel has almost emptied. In the lobby the French housekeeper is shouting, "Everyone has gone. It is the end of the war, good God. My cashier — this man over here — he says he wants to shoot himself. Thank goodness he has no gun. Please, should I laugh or cry?" It is a question I am about to ask myself. So much for Bing Crosby.

I return to my room in a manner of flying, gather my type-

THE LAST DAY

writer, radio and notes and jam them into one small bag; the
rest I leave. Where the hell did I hide my money? On top of the
cistern, of course. Two room attendants arrive and view my
frantic packing, bemused and slightly in awe. One of them
asks, "Are you checking out, sir?" I say that I am, in a manner
of speaking. "But your laundry won't be back till this evening,
sir." I try not to look at him. "Please ... you keep it ... and
anything else you see."

I push a bundle of piastres into their hands, knowing that I
am buying their deference in the face of my graceless exit.
After ten years, what a way to leave. But that I want to leave is
beyond question; I have had my fill of the war.

The French housekeeper has her face in her hands as I streak
by. Inexplicably, I experience a fleeting moment of guilt about
the unpaid bill; but I owe them for only two nights and if, as she
says, the cashier wants to shoot himself, he will be in no mood
to receive my money.

Outside, three policemen are dragging large coils of barbed
wire across the footpath. One of them shouts something at me,
probably about the bill. Lam Son Square is empty, except for
soldiers slouched in doorways and in the gutter. One of them is
walking briskly up Tu Do, shouting at me; he looks drunk; he
unholsters his revolver, rests it on an unsteady arm, takes aim
and fires. The bullet sings by me; I run in a circle.

"Hey, where the bloody hell is everybody?" The Antipodean
accent belongs to my old friend George James, with whom I
worked my apprenticeship in this trade some seventeen years
ago on the *Sydney Daily Telegraph*. George is now a television
director with the Canadian Broadcasting Corporation and he
and his crew have just returned from filming at Tan Son Nhut,
and now wish, like I, to leave. They have a jeep, whose driver is
heaving with fear.

"Number 35 Gia Long Street," we tell the driver.

"What is that, please?" he says.

"We hope it's a building with a helicopter on the roof."

"I see ... okay, I drive you if you take me with you."

The jeep goes in a wide circle and we quickly realize that if
No. 35 Gia Long exists, it will be deserted by now. We tell him
to take us to the American embassy.

THE LAST DAY

There is a crowd pressing at the gate of the embassy; some are merely the curious who have come to watch the Americans' mighty aerial Dunkirk, but there are many who grip the bars and plead with the Marine guard to let them in and wave wax-sealed documents and letters from American officials saying what wonderful and patriotic people they are. An old man has a letter from Sergeant Trabert P. Travers who a long time ago ran the bar at the Air Force officers' club in Pleiku, which I will remember for its great plastic chandeliers, best California wines and Filipino waiters in white evening jackets. The old man used to wash dishes there, and his note from Sergeant Travers, dated June 5, 1967, says, "Mr. Nha, the bearer of this letter, faithfully served the cause of freedom in the Republic of Vietnam." Mr. Nha also produces a toy Texas Ranger's star which one of the pilots at Pleiku gave him. He waves the letter and the toy Texas Ranger's star at the Marine guard who is shouting at the crowd. "Now, please don't panic . . . please!" For as long as they can remember, these people, who worked for the Americans, have been told to fear the Communists because of all the barbaric things Communists are supposed to do; now they are being told, with the Communists in their backyards, that they should not panic. Their confusion is complete.

The old man attempts to slide through the opening in the gate and is pushed to the ground by the Marine telling them not to panic. He gets up, tries again, and is tackled by a second Marine who propels him outside with the butt of his rifle and hurls the Texas Ranger's badge over the heads of the crowd and screws the letter from Sergeant Trabert P. Travers into a ball. As I struggle through the crowd, pushing and using my strength in order to get my free ride away from the war, I feel only shame.

Inside the embassy compound the Marines and the cowboys are standing around the stump of the great tamarind tree. "Okay, you tell me what we're gonna do about this immovable bastard," says one of the cowboys into his walkie-talkie. "Take it easy, Jed," comes the reply, "just you and the boys level it down by at least another foot, so there's plenty of room for the rotors."

Saigon begins to fall. On April 28 the city was bombed, which was the beginning of the end of thirty years of war. UNITED PRESS INTERNATIONAL

THE LAST DAY

"And Jed..."

"Yeah?"

"Get all those shavings swept up, or sure as hell they're gonna be sucked into the engines..."

So the Marines and the cowboys go on swinging their axes at the stump, but with such mounting frustration and incompetence that their chopping becomes an entertainment for those both inside and outside the gate, and especially for the grinning French guards on the high wall of the French embassy next door. The French, who came to Vietnam a century ago as thieves, are clearly amused by the humiliating antics of those who came as mere salesmen, spending billions of dollars and thousands of lives on a campaign of hard-sell, and, in the end, selling nothing.

"Now I want to make this very clear to you," says Marine Colonel Summers, through a bullhorn. "Every one of you folks is going to get out of here. Let me repeat that. All you people here with us today are going to be flown to safety and freedom. Not one of you will be left behind. I will go only after the last one of you has left. And the United States Ambassador has assured me he will leave right at the end, after you and me. On that we give you our solemn word." Colonel Summers is the Marine officer in charge of co-ordinating the evacuation from the embassy. He gets down from the soft-drink stall, where he has addressed them, and walks slowly through the people crowded on the lawn around the swimming pool, saying, "Now don't you worry"... "Sure you'll get a job in the States," as though he has taken it upon himself to sweep up some of the dust of America's honor in Vietnam. He is, it is clear to me, a man of honor and of compassion, which are qualities unknown to many of those to whom he has just given his word.

There is in Vietnamese, a language given much to poetry and irony, a saying that "only when the house burns, do you see the faces of the rats." Over there is a general who was a heroin trader, who used his officers as dealers and gave many of his own men the habit; and over there is the corrupt Dr. Phan Quang Dan, former deputy prime minister and minister responsible for social welfare and refugee resettlement, a man seen by Washington and by Ambassador Martin as the em-

THE LAST DAY

bodiment of the true nationalist spirit of South Vietnam. Dr. Dan, an obsessive anti-Communist who was constantly making speeches exhorting his countrymen to stand and fight, is surrounded by his family — his plump wife sweltering under a fur coat — and by a platoon of bagmen, whose bags never leave their grip; it is not difficult to suppose what is in them. Over there, being fanned by a servant, is Mr. Nguyen Ba Can, speaker of the lower house of the National Assembly and briefly prime minister, known also for his corruption and subservience to ex-President Thieu. These are men who for years called on the people of South Vietnam to sacrifice everything for the "salvation of the fatherland" and who will fill seats on the helicopters while the soldiers they have abandoned continue to die in order to preserve the officials' escape route.

The "beautiful people" of Saigon are also here, including those young men of military age whose wealthy parents paid large bribes to keep them out of the army. Although these young men would be listed as soldiers on some unit's roster, they would never report for duty and their commanding officer would pocket their wages. These "ghost soldiers," as they were called, continued to lead the good life in Saigon; in the cafés, on their Hondas, beside the pool at the Cercle Sportif, while the sons of the poor fought and died in futility at Quang Tri, An Loc, Xuan Loc and all the other sacrificial places.

"Look, it is me . . . let me in, please . . . thank you very much . . . hello, it is me!"

The shrill voice at the back of the crowd outside the gate belongs to Lieutenant General Dang Van Quang, regarded by his countrymen and by many Americans to be one of the biggest and richest profiteers in South Vietnam. The Marine guard has a list of people he can let in, and General Quang is on it. With great care, the guard helps General Quang, who is very fat, over the fifteen-foot bars and then retrieves his three Samsonite bags. The general is so relieved to be inside that he walks away, leaving his twenty-year-old son to struggle hopelessly in the crowd. "I do hope he will be all right," he says, still panting as he receives the welcoming handshake of an embassy official. "You know, I have sent two children to Australia, three to Canada and one to Paris. I would have sent *him* out of the

THE LAST DAY

country, but he was of draft age and, as I told my wife, I didn't want to do anything that was against the law."

There are two packets of dollars sagging from his jacket breast pocket. When they are pointed out to him, he stuffs them back in, and laughs. To the Americans, General Quang is known as "Giggles" and "General Fats." When he was commander of South Vietnamese troops in the Mekong Delta a few years ago, his reputation became such that President Thieu had to dismiss him. This was a great blow to Mrs. Quang (now in Guam), who ran brothels in the Delta. When asked why he continued to employ Giggles Quang as an adviser, Thieu laughed and said, "I like to have him around, so I know what he's doing."

Albert Steinberg does not have the same friends as General Quang. Albert, a construction worker, is in the crowd outside when the general is eased over the gate. Albert has managed to get to the bars of the gate and waves his American passport under the nose of the Marine guard. "Hey, what about me?" he pleads. "Come on, guys, I'm an American. Let me in, will you?" Loren Jenkins, the correspondent of *Newsweek,* attempts to go to his rescue by leading an embassy official right up to Albert's face. "This man's an American," says Jenkins, "will you get him inside!" The official looks at his anxious countryman, drags on a cigarette and walks away.

Among the Americans luckier than Albert there is a festive spirit. They squat on the lawn around the swimming pool with champagne in ice buckets looted from the embassy restaurant, and they whoop it up; one man in a big Western hat sprays bubbly on another and there is joyous singing by two aircraft mechanics, Frank and Elmer. Over and over they sing, to the tune of the Camptown Races . . .

> We're going home in freedom birds,
> Doo dah, doo dah;
> We ain't goin' home in plastic bags,
> Oh doo dah day.

"This is where I've come after ten years," says Warren Parker, almost in tears. "See that man over there? He's a National Police official . . . nothing better than a torturer . . . scum." Warren Parker was, until this morning, United States

Consul in My Tho, in the Delta, where I met him last week. He is a quiet, bashful man who has spent ten years in Vietnam trying to "advise" the Vietnamese and puzzling why so many of them did not seem to want his or his government's advice. Parker and I push our way into the restaurant beside the swimming pool, past a man on the door saying, "No Veeetnamese in here, no Veeetnamese," and we loot a chilled bottle of Taylor New York State wine, pink and sweet. The glasses have already gone, so we share the bottle. "I'll tell you something," he says in his soft Georgia accent, "if there ever was a moment of truth for me, it's today. All these years I've been down there, doing a job of work for my country and for this country, and today all I can see is that we've succeeded in separating all the good people from the scum."

2:05 p.m.

The first Jolly Green Giant helicopter arrives at Tan Son Nhut; the Jolly Green Giant must be the first aircraft to be named after a brand of frozen peas. General Curry of the Marines runs from beneath the rotors and wants to know why the other thirty-five Jolly Green Giants and Chinooks and Sea Stallions are not right behind him. When General Smith tells him that someone gave a phony order, he turns crimson with anger.

With the arrival of the first evacuation helicopter there is

American officials (above) try to force back the crowd outside the American Embassy on April 29, the last day. LOREN JENKINS, NEWSWEEK

THE LAST DAY

pandemonium among the people waiting in the bowling alley and the gymnasium. These are the people who swarmed onto the runway when the two C-130s attempted to land, whose panic put an end to any hope of an orderly evacuation by conventional aircraft. Many will not get out, because there are not enough seats and their American "sponsors" know it. So, swiftly and unceremoniously, big men slip away from their "fiancées" and their families, even from women with whom they have lived for years, some even from wives and children. It is every "round eye" for himself now.

In the meantime, most of the American and "TCN" Press have joined a final, macabre tour of Saigon. The coded signal to evacuate was not the boo-boo-boo of Bing but the inscrutable announcement that "Mother wants you to call her . . ." When word of the evacuation spread (but not to me), the journalists streamed out of the Caravelle, the Continental Palace, the Miramar, the Peninsular, the Palace and the Majestic hotels and marched to the first assembly point, an apartment block opposite the Bank of America, where they found not a helicopter on the roof, but a growing crowd of Vietnamese who obviously had decided that if they stayed with the foreigners they also would get out. From there they marched to the assembly point at No. 35 Gia Long and found a padlocked door and a faded sign saying, UNIVERSITY OF MARYLAND, SAIGON EDUCATION CENTER. Finally, three vintage buses arrived and those who were quick got on them. The buses were driven by Americans who had never before driven a bus and who did not know their way in Saigon. After a long, circuitous tour of the city, followed by car loads of people pleading to be taken on board, including two Vietnamese lawyers dressed in their court costumes of black robes and white tabs, the buses reached Tan Son Nhut, where they were fired on by South Vietnamese soldiers. At this, the Marine escort in the first bus called frantically into his walkie-talkie, "Dodge City control, this is Wagon Master. What's the situation at the gate?" The reply was immediate: "Bust it, if necessary!"

They reached Dodge City.

But a fourth bus did not make it to Dodge City. On board this bus was Keyes Beech, the veteran Asian correspondent of the

THE LAST DAY

Chicago Daily News, who filed this memorable report . . . "We heard the bad news over the driver's radio on the way out: 'Security conditions are out of control at Tan Son Nhut. Do not go to Tan Son Nhut. Repeat, do not go to Tan Son Nhut' . . . It was two p.m. when we headed back to the city. Nobody on that bus will ever forget the next few hours . . . We were a bus load of fools piloted by a man who had never driven a bus and had to wire the ignition when it stalled because the Vietnamese driver had run away with the keys the night before. 'I'm doing the best I can,' said Bill Austin of Miami, Oklahoma, the man at the wheel, as we careened through narrow streets, knocking over sidewalk vendors, side-swiping passing vehicles and sending Vietnamese scattering like leaves in the wind. [One of the buses knocked a baby out of his mother's arms and killed him.]

"At every stop Vietnamese beat on the doors and windows pleading to be let inside. We merely looked at them . . . Every time we opened the door, we had to beat and kick them back. For no reason, except that we were following another bus, we went to the Saigon port area, one of the toughest parts of the city, where the crowds were uglier than elsewhere . . . I got off the bus and went over to John Moore, the embassy security officer who was sitting in one of those sedans with the flashy blinker on top. 'Do you know why we are here and what you are going to do with us?' I asked him. Moore shrugged help-lessly. 'There are ships,' he said, gesturing toward sandbagged Vietnamese vessels lying alongside the dock. I looked around at the gathering crowd. Small boys were snatching typewriters and bags of film. This, as the Chinese would say, looked like a bad joss. I didn't know how or whether I was going to get out of Saigon, but I damned well knew I wasn't going to stay here. I got back on the bus . . . I found myself pushing a middle-aged Vietnamese woman who had been sitting beside me and had asked me to look after her because she worked for the Americans and the Vietcong would cut her throat. That's what they all said, and maybe they are right. But she fought her way back to my side. 'Why did you push me?' she asked. I had no answer.

"Austin [the driver] didn't know what to do with us so we drove to the American Embassy. There the Vietnamese

THE LAST DAY

woman decided to get off. 'I have worked for the United States Government for ten years,' she said, 'but you do not trust me and I do not trust you. Even if we do get to Tan Son Nhut, they wouldn't let me on the plane.' She was right, of course. 'I am going home and poison myself,' she said. I didn't say anything because there was nothing to say.

"There was only one way inside [the embassy]: through the crowd and over the ten-foot wall. Once we moved into that seething mass we ceased to be correspondents. We were only men fighting for our lives, scratching, clawing, pushing even closer to that wall . . . We were like animals. Now, I thought, I know what it's like to be a Vietnamese. I am one of them. But if I could get over the wall I would be an American again.

"Somebody grabbed my sleeve and wouldn't let go. I turned my head and looked into the face of a Vietnamese youth. 'You adopt me and take me with you and I'll help you,' he screamed. 'If you don't, you don't go.' I said I'd adopt him. I'd have said anything. Could this be happening to me? Suddenly my arm was free, and I edged closer to the wall. There was a pair of Marines on the wall. They were trying to help us and kick the Vietnamese down. One of them looked down at me. 'Help me,' I pleaded. 'Please help me.'

"That Marine helped me. He reached down with his long, muscular arm and pulled me up as if I were a helpless child. I lay on a tin roof gasping for breath like a landed fish . . . God bless the Marines. I was one myself in the last of the just wars. One American offered me a cup of water and a doctor asked me if I wanted a tranquilizer. I accepted the water and declined the tranquilizer."

3:00 p.m.

The first evacuation helicopters land at Tan Son Nhut, and a Marine at the head of the queue barks, "No baggage!" Typewriters, radios, cameras are left. A nun from the Good Shepherd Convent says, "I sent 100 children out here yesterday, but they had to turn back because of rockets. I do wish I could get them to the States. I pray one day I shall . . ." Such is her second faith: that it is better for Vietnamese to become Americans rather than to remain Vietnamese, as is their birthright, if it

THE LAST DAY

means living under a government which she and America do not like. She gathers in her habit and runs to the helicopter.

Over Fire Base "Snuffy," Tay Ninh province, South Vietnam, August 30, 1970

"You could say the helicopter has been our salvation in this war," says Captain Frank Littlewood, from Cleveland, Ohio. "Why, you could say that without the helicopter we wouldn't be doing so damn well in this war!" Captain Littlewood is a Psy-Ops officer of the US First Air Cavalry Division whose colors include the crossed swords of Custer's Seventh Cavalry. (Psy-Ops means Psychological Warfare.)

"What we're doing today," shouts Captain Littlewood over the noise of the rotors, "is psyching out the enemy. We're going to play a tape we call Wandering Soul. Now you've got to understand the Vietnamese way of life to realize the power behind Wandering Soul. You see, the Vietnamese people worship their ancestors and they take a lot of notice of the spirits and stuff like that. Well, what we're going to do is fly low over the jungle and broadcast the voices of ancestors — you know, ghosts — which we've simulated in our studios. Got it? These ghosts — these ancestors, I mean — are going to tell the Vietcong to stop messing with the people's right to live freely, or they're going to disown them."

Our helicopter drops to a few hundred feet above the trees, Captain Littlewood throws a switch and a reverberating voice emits from two loudspeakers. While the voice reverberates and occasionally hoots, a sergeant hurls out handfuls of leaflets which also offer ancestral threats. Captain Littlewood himself hurls out one unopened box of leaflets. "Maybe," he says, "I'll hit one Cong on the head and we won't have to worry about changing his mind."

3:15 p.m.

Graham Martin strides out of the lift, through the lobby of the embassy and into the compound. The big helicopters have yet to arrive and the stump of the tamarind is not noticeably shorter, in spite of the Marines' and cowboys' furious, though erratic, chopping and sawing. His Cadillac is waiting for him

See overleaf. An American official says goodbye to Vietnam. UNITED PRESS INTERNATIONAL

THE LAST DAY

and Eddie the bodyguard opens the door, which bangs against the grenades hanging on the breast of his flak jacket. With embassy staff looking on incredulously, the Cadillac drives toward the gate, which is now under siege from a thousand people. The Marine at the gate cannot believe his eyes. The Cadillac stops, the Marine throws his arms into the air and the Cadillac reverses. The Ambassador gets out and storms past the stump and the cowboys, with Eddie trailing behind. "I am going to walk once more to my residence," he says to himself. "I shall walk freely in this city. I shall leave Vietnam when the President tells me to leave." He leaves the embassy by a side entrance, forces his own way through the crowd and walks the four blocks to his house — trailed, of course, by Eddie. An hour and a half later he returns with his poodle, Nitnoy, and his Vietnamese manservant.

People are now beginning to come over the wall. The Marines, who have orders not to use their guns, have been up all night and are doped with "speed" — methedrine — which provides a "high" of twenty-four hours before the body craves sleep. But methedrine also whittles the nerve ends, and some of the young Marines are beginning to show the effects. As the first Chinook helicopter makes its precarious landing, its rotors slash into a tree, and the snapping branches sound like gunfire. "Down! Down!" screams a Marine corporal to the line of people crouched against the wall, waiting their turn to be evacuated, until an officer comes and calms him.

The helicopter's capacity is fifty, but it lifts off with seventy. The pilot's skill is breathtaking as he climbs vertically to two hundred feet, with bullets pinging against the rotors, and the confetti of twenty-one years of illusions playing in the downdraft. Some of the embassy's documents, which have been shredded, have been left in the compound in large, open plastic bags, a prey to the slightest breeze. These documents, going back to 1954, were once secret reports from ambassadors and cables from Presidents and memoranda from CIA men, and those that the shredder could not shred have been burned. An embassy official has told an American television reporter that maybe five million dollars in cash have been burned and that every safe in the embassy has been emptied and locked again,

People storm the American Embassy on the last day, but the Marines fight them off.
NIK WHEELER. SIPA PRESS

THE LAST DAY

"just to fool the gooks." Indeed, charred fifty-dollar bills swirl with the confetti.

5:27 p.m.

It is shortly before dawn in Washington. The President is awake and calls the White House switchboard to ask if there are any calls. "All is very quiet, sir," is the reply. The President gets out of bed and touches his toes twenty times. Yesterday he touched them thirty times; his morning glass of buttermilk arrives.

As the President of the United States touches his toes and sips his buttermilk, two Marines watch a young girl struggle through the barbed wire on the wall of the embassy in Saigon. At first they do nothing, just wait patiently for her hands to claw the last few inches. Then one of them brings his rifle butt down on her left hand, crushing it, and the other brings his boot down on her right hand, again and again. The girl falls, crying, back into the mob.

Somehow, most of one family have managed to get over the wall: a man, his wife, and her father. Their son of about twelve and his grandmother are next, but the barrel of an M-16 rifle spins them back to the other side. The wife pleads with a Marine to let the rest of her family over, but he does not hear her; he has fixed his bayonet and lunges it at the boy's neck.

Chicago, August 29, 1968

It is eight o'clock on a warm summer's night. About one hour from now, in the National Amphitheater, which is surrounded by pig pens and stockyards and by police and soldiers with fixed bayonets, the Democratic Party will choose Hubert Humphrey as its candidate for President, Lyndon Johnson having announced his abdication in April over the issue of Vietnam.

I have moved back into the street, among the crowd, and there is a soldier pushing a bayonet into a young man's chest. He pushes it almost delicately until their eyes meet and they both fall silent. "Now will you move!" says the soldier; and the young man, who has come here to demonstrate against the war in Vietnam, rips away his shirt and looks at the blood trickling from his chest. A photographer and I take his arm and say he

THE LAST DAY

will be all right; then a policeman takes him, puts him in the paddy wagon and clubs him unconscious. And while he lies there, the photographer is also knocked down, in a litter of lenses and film rolls, and the same club is swung unsuccessfully at me.

Across the street, near the Conrad Hilton Hotel, "the largest and friendliest on earth," a line of policemen is marching and chanting obscenities, their baby-blue helmets and plexiglass face-shields glinting in the television lights, their paunches swathed in revolvers and canisters of tear gas and Mace. Then they run, their pinky faces flushed with the excitement of having sighted their prey: a dozen young people, mostly helpers of Humphrey's rival, Senator Eugene McCarthy, who have been staying at the hotel and have come out to watch. The young people see what is about to happen to them, but see nowhere they can run. So they group together against the plate-glass window, some of them on their knees; and they are pummelled through the window and kicked through the glass.

Almost every family in the United States with a television set will have seen scenes like this, and the National Guardsman pushing a grenade launcher through the window of a car and saying to two students, "Get out or I'll let you have this," and the people staggering, retching through the gas. Senator McCarthy has turned his hotel room into a field station, but even those helping the wounded are beaten in the corridor. The senator sits on the edge of his bed and says to reporters, "I just want to say this to America. If we _ever_ get out of Vietnam, if this war ever ends, it will be because of these young people who belong to another America, who had the courage to come to Chicago today."

5:30 p.m.

The swishing of the rotors now drowns the sounds of the dusk: the crump of artillery, the gunfire, the cries of women attempting to push young children over the wall. At least a thousand people are still inside the embassy, waiting to be evacuated, although most of the big names, like General "Giggles" Quang, have seen themselves onto the first helicopters; the rest of their countrymen in the embassy compound are mostly those con-

THE LAST DAY

ditioned to be afraid and they wait almost passively, almost stunned.

Inside the embassy itself there is champagne foaming onto polished desks, and remarkable moments as some of the embassy staff try to systematically wreck their own offices: smashing water coolers, pouring bottles of Scotch into the carpets, sweeping pictures from the wall. In a third-floor office a picture of the late President Johnson is delivered into a wastepaper basket, while a framed quotation from Lawrence of Arabia is left on the wall, no doubt a reflection of one man's frustration. The quotation reads, "Better to let them do it imperfectly, than to do it perfectly yourself, for it is their country, their war, and your time is short."

From the third floor I can see the British embassy across the road. It is being quietly ransacked now; the Union Jack spread across the main entrance, no doubt to ward off evil spirits, has been torn away and looters are at work with little interference from the police. I derive some small satisfaction from the sight of this. It was here last Friday that the British Ambassador, a spiffy chap named John Bushell, shredded his own papers and mounted his own pathetic little evacuation after refusing to take with him a dozen very frightened British passport holders. Before he drove away, I had a chat with Mr. Bushell. "We are pulling out for reasons of safety," he said. "Our main responsibility is the safety of the British community in Saigon." I said fine, but what about those people who waved their British passports outside the gates of the British embassy at half past seven this morning and they were not even allowed into the compound? "Look here," he replied, "we gave ample warning. We put advertisements in the local papers. The trouble with these people, as I understand it, was that they didn't have tax clearance, which takes ten days, as well as exit visas from the Vietnamese government." Exit visas? Tax clearances? But wasn't this an emergency evacuation for reasons, as he had just said, of protecting life? "Well, yes," he replied, "but we really can't break the rules laid down by a government, can we?" But surely this government virtually did not exist and tomorrow there might be anarchy and a great deal of danger here, which was why he was getting out? "That may be true," said the

THE LAST DAY

Ambassador, "but we gave these people a reasonable time to get the paperwork done, and you really can't expect us to help them at such short notice . . . look here, the Americans surely will pick up any stray palefaces." But, I pointed out, these were Indians and Chinese. "Oh, Hong Kongers . . ." he replied. But weren't they asking for help? "They should have heeded our warnings . . . they'll just have to work hard at it, won't they?" I then went on to ask the Ambassador why a member of his staff announced on Wednesday that some Vietnamese staff were being left behind because they could not get exit visas in time. At this, he turned to another British official and said, "How many coolies are left, do you know?" The official replied, "Coolies? Oh, about thirty-six in all." By "coolies" they meant the Vietnamese. The attitude of the British Ambassador was not, of course, a harmless relic of the Raj. His sentiments are shared by many of those who have served Her Majesty in Saigon since the Geneva conference divided Vietnam twenty-one years ago. Indeed, it has been difficult to know why Britain has bothered to send diplomats to Saigon at all, for their job has been to adhere to and to help shore up the American view of Indochina and the war, to assist with the import of Scotch whisky and banknotes and to otherwise remain in their diplomatic cocoon: keeping cool in the fine British Club pool, playing darts on Saturdays with Americans and Australians. The extent of British complicity in the American war has never been fully understood in Britain or America. The British fought the war in their special way. Hovercraft were supplied secretly to the Americans — the same hovercraft which killed aimlessly along the rivers of the Delta — together with helicopter radio equipment and jungle training facilities for the Green Berets, with whom the British Strategic Air Services (the SAS) played secret games. With the knowledge and approval of the British Government, President Nixon used bombs stored in Britain in his attempts to flatten Hanoi during the terror raids of Christmas, 1972. Appropriately, the last British act in Vietnam — unless one counts Ambassador Bushell's cheerio to his "coolies" — was Prime Minister Wilson's dispatch of a frigate into the South China Sea at the request of Washington. Fortunately, no one paid it much notice.

THE LAST DAY

6:15 p.m.

It is time to catch my Jolly Green Giant. Lights blinking, it descends into the compound, and we are told by Colonel Summers, "Now . . . go . . . move!" The loadmaster stops counting at sixty; people are in each other's arms. The helicopter tilts, climbs and there are shots; and I am immediately back in time to the years the Americans took us all to the war in their helicopters so that we could have a grandstand view of their catastrophe; in the morning they would fly you to watch American artillery blasting away at villages and American planes dropping napalm on people, and in the evening they would bring you back to a large base camp where more than likely there was a Press room and a padded bar, with soft lights, pretty girls and a jukebox. It did not matter if you were friend or foe then, and it does not matter now. Such are they.

We fly over the center of the city, over the presidential palace where "Big" Minh awaits his fate, and the Caravelle Hotel, where I owe for two days and have left my only black shoes — and, I have just realized, my preciously collected Vietnam file of ten years; well, it's all out of date now; the story is closing down.

We fly out along the Saigon River, over the Rung Sat, the "swamp of death" which lies between the city and the sea. The two gunners scan the ground, as they always used to, looking for "Charlie." Some of us have on our minds the memory of the heat-seeking missile that brought a helicopter down as we watched this morning. There is some fire around us, and it is probably from ARVN soldiers firing more out of frustration than anger; but they, and the victors, are letting us go; and when the South China Sea is beneath us, the pilot, who is so young he has acne and who is red-eyed with fatigue, lights up a cigarette and hands the packet around, and we smile and feel much relieved. In the back there is a reminder of what we have left: a woman, who has left her daughter on the other side of the embassy wall, cries softly.

Below us now is an armada of craft of every kind: sanpans, barges, tugs, fishing trawlers, landing craft, tramp steamers, tankers, warships. One ship is burning and someone has said it

British Ambassador to South Vietnam, John Bushell, waves bye-bye to his "coolies" on the day he left Saigon. JACQUES PAVLOVSKY, SYGMA

THE LAST DAY

is to light the way for the helicopters, which sounds ridiculous but may well be true.

It is an hour and a half's flying to the carrier *Midway,* and when we touch down there is another helicopter ahead of us, landing drunkenly on the deck, spilling out women, children and a Honda motorcycle. The South Vietnamese Air Force has come home at last; and as the pilots and their families disperse, the helicopters, each of which cost the American people half a million dollars, are pushed unceremoniously overboard, like giant extinct fish; or perhaps obsolete Fords is a better description. "The only one we've kept," says a Marine officer, "is the one that brought Air Vice Marshal Ky." So Ky is here: Nguyen Cao Ky, the man who just a week ago at a mass rally in Saigon told everybody to stand and fight and called those who fled "cowards"; the man who, as President and Vice President under Thieu, used the American Army to brutally put down political opposition in Hue. Apparently he arrived as dapper as ever, in a spotless white uniform with only one decoration.

"Okay, turkey, go around again, turkey . . . try again . . . take it nice and easy, turkey." The Vietnamese major who has flown a Cessna aircraft out to the *Midway* has never landed on an aircraft carrier. He circles and circles, then flies straight at the ship, dipping for a moment beneath the deck line, then landing perfectly. "Hey, how about that?" he says with an American accent. "First time ever and I didn't goof it!" His plane is then thrown into the sea.

9:30 p.m.

The business day has begun in Washington and Henry Kissinger calls the President to say that the evacuation from Tan Son Nhut has been completed, but there is mounting concern for those still in the embassy. Kissinger suggests he order Ambassador Martin to "wrap it up and get his ass out of there." The President, who is about to receive King Hussein, agrees. He also asks Kissinger to listen to the draft of his message to the nation "concluding the war in Vietnam." The President's message to the nation asks Americans to close ranks and to put Vietnam behind them. It suggests that political lessons have been learned, it says nothing about moral lessons.

South Vietnamese pilots flew their helicopters to the American evacuation fleet. Each helicopter, which had cost the American taxpayers half a million dollars, was pushed overboard. MATHEW NAYTHONS, SIPA PRESS

THE LAST DAY

Kissinger calls Martin at the embassy, but the Ambassador cannot come to the phone. He is in the swimming pool area where the rest of the "endangered Vietnamese" are still waiting their turn. There is another champagne wake under way in the office of special assistant Conrad LaGueux. Everyone is there except Martin. Kissinger leaves a message.

The loading zone is lit by the headlights of embassy cars and the big helicopters are now taking up to ninety people, thirty more than their capacity. Martin calls Kissinger, who says the President wants his ass out of there. Martin passes this to Martin Garrett, the head of security, who gathers all the remaining Americans together. The Vietnamese around the swimming pool sense what is happening and try to surge through the narrow gate into the landing zone area. The Marines stop them, and Colonel Summers appears once again to reassure them; he cannot believe that Washington will allow the Ambassador to leave without them. Outside the wall, a grenade explodes in the crowd and a Marine reports on his walkie-talkie, "Many wounded here." There is no one to help them.

11:30 p.m.

It is a crisp, sunny morning in Marshalltown, Iowa. Henry Judge has almost finished his postman's round when the black Chevrolet with two Marine officers pulls into the curb and one of them calls him over. They speak for a few minutes, then shake hands. They have told him that his boy, Darwin, was one of the last two Americans to die in Vietnam.

The reporters arrive half an hour later and they find Henry still delivering letters. "I guess I'm kind of stunned," he says. They walk with him to his big old clapboard house and wait outside while he tells his wife. Some time later they both come out on the porch and Mrs. Judge says without tears, "All I can say is that he felt he had to be there to keep the Communists from coming here. We're proud of that boy. We're good Christian folk, you see, and the good Lord'll take care of us. I love my boy, but when it's your time to go . . ."

12:00 Midnight

It is noon in Washington and Henry Kissinger stands up at a

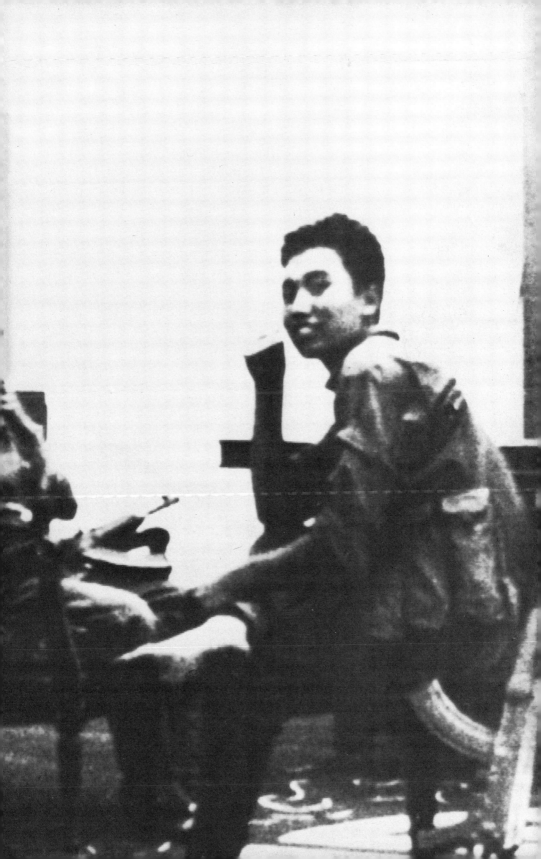

THE LAST DAY

State Department briefing and says that Americans were forced to flee from a country in which they had fought for twenty-one years because the North Vietnamese "changed signals" two nights ago. "We thought a negotiated settlement was highly probable then," he says, "but they switched to the military option..." Kissinger's voice has the ring of a man laying out yet one last excuse, without first taking the trouble to convince himself. His guttural voice is so quiet, so sepulchral, it almost trails away; he allows only a few questions, then hurries away. From the same rostrum two and half years ago he announced, on his return from his "greatest triumph" in Paris, that peace was at hand in Vietnam: "peace with honor." Today both peace and defeat are at hand.

2:30 a.m.

Kissinger calls Martin and tells him to end the evacuation at precisely 3:45 a.m. Martin pleads for an extension of three quarters of an hour. Kissinger says he will call him back. Kissinger puts down the telephone and interrupts the President at a meeting with Congressmen from the western states who are much concerned about sheep farmers' problems with coyotes. The President agrees to the extension, but not a minute more; he is growing impatient with the Ambassador. Kissinger calls Martin back and tells him. Martin remains in his office alone and for a while no one disturbs him. An autographed photograph of Richard Nixon — "With my thanks" — is on the wall behind him. After half an hour he emerges with an attaché case, a suit bag and the Stars and Stripes folded in a carrier bag. He meets Tom Polgar, George Jacobson and Conrad LaGueux at the lift and they go in silence to the sixth floor where a helicopter is waiting.

4:30 a.m.

"Lady Ace 09 is in the air with Code Two." "Code Two" is the code for an American Ambassador. The clipped announcement over the tied circuit means that twenty-one years of American presence in Indochina has officially and irrevocably ended. His helicopter banks over Highway One, the main road into Saigon from the north-east, which is ablaze with the headlights

See previous page. Vietcong soldiers celebrate their victory in Saigon in the office of former President Thieu. HOANG VAN CUONG, UNITED PRESS INTERNATIONAL

THE LAST DAY

of trucks of the North Vietnamese Army.

5:00 a.m.

Martin Garrett asks Colonel Summers to get all the Marines inside the embassy building. Summers says there are still more than 500 Vietnamese waiting to be evacuated. Garrett replies that the pilots have been flying for fourteen hours and the President has said that the evacuation must end. He says to tell the Marines to walk slowly, casually, back to the embassy lobby and then to lock the door to the stairwell behind them. This they do, and at that moment people stream over the wall, and past the stump of the great tamarind tree and the embassy cars with their engines running and their headlights on.

Dawn is breaking as the last Marines reach the roof and fire tear gas canisters into the stairwell. They can hear the smashing of glass and desperate attempts to break open the empty safes. The Marines are exhausted and beginning to panic; the last helicopter has yet to arrive. They fire Mace, the gas which disables muscles, into the stairwell. Colonel Summers can still see people waiting in a long, orderly queue around the swimming pool, still believing that their turn for evacuation will come, because he has told them again and again that he will not leave without them. Even the firemen, who have worked for twelve hours to protect the helicopters, are still at their posts; he gave the same pledge to them. But now he is going without them, having learned only by accident that the Ambassador left an hour ago. "I will be the last man to leave this embassy," Graham Martin had told him in his office. "You have my solemn word on that."

When he lands on the *USS Blue Ridge*, the Seventh Fleet command ship, Colonel Summers is still crying.

About the Author

John Pilger, reporter and broadcaster, is the London *Daily Mirror's* chief foreign correspondent. He has reported most major world news events of the last decade, and has been a war correspondent four times over. But his most consistent and evocative writing has come from Vietnam, where the war still had ten years to run when he first went there, and from the United States, where he has reported the deepening disillusionment, the deceptions and the agony of America's coming defeat at the hands of a small, underdeveloped Asian country.

John Pilger returned to Vietnam in the spring of 1975. In *The Last Day* he is a witness to the total humiliation of the world's greatest military power in the space of one long, brutal and bitterly farcical day — April 29, 1975 — the day the Americans escaped from Vietnam, the day the American empire in South East Asia collapsed.

On that historic day, only a handful of reporters were in the besieged American embassy in Saigon, once the fortress-like symbol of American might, and Pilger was one of them. In *The Last Day* he recounts, hour by hour, the last act of the longest American war; and at the same time he recalls events and images and characters from the years he has known Vietnam.

John Pilger arrived in Britain thirteen years ago from Australia, where he learned his journalism on the Sydney *Daily* and *Sunday Telegraph*. He has won five British awards for his reporting. Among these, the top award of Journalist of the Year and the award of International Reporter of the Year were chiefly for his work from Vietnam and America. He has made two television documentaries about Vietnam, both of them prize winners at international festivals. Shortly before he left to report the end of the war, he was named News Reporter of the Year. The citation read: "His material is factual, but his expression of it powerfully emotional, and his contribution to present-day news reporting unsurpassed." He is married to journalist Scarth Flett, and they have a three-year-old son, Sam.